It's My Party and I'll Lie If I Want To

The "Plus Truss" edition

MIKE CASHMAN

and

AUGUSTA LEES

Viewdelta Press

GW00503614

Cover design and photo by Mike Cashman, incorporating quotations from *FINDINGS OF SECOND PERMANENT SECRETARY'S INVESTIGATION INTO ALLEGED GATHERINGS ON GOVERNMENT PREMISES DURING COVID RESTRICTIONS 25 MAY 2022*, (also known as the "Sue Gray Report"), which is available from the UK Government website, quotations from Boris Johnson answering questions in Parliament, and also incorporating cartoon of Boris Johnson with thanks for the image by **Succo** from **Pixabay.com**

Published by Viewdelta Press
First edition September 2022
Second ("Plus Truss") edition November 2022
ISBN 978 1 9162486 8 7
Viewdelta IMPL202211130211Q6

- Mike Cashman and Augusta Lees -

What Will You Find in This book?

Now MPs all whoever you may be,
If you want to rise to the top of the tree,
You can treat the electorate as if they're fools
If you're not constrained by the normal Rules
(He's not constrained by the normal Rules).
So, don't hold me to anything I'll say,
'Cos I'm Prime Minister of all UK.
(So, don't hold him to anything he'll say,
'Cos He's Prime Minister of all
UK).
*- The final verse of "Prime
Minister of all UK",
by Mike Cashman,*

She had air-time,
Lost her grip on power. (Already)
Those journos had their finest hour. (In 5 minutes)
Local Radio. (Worth the license fee alone)

All is clear, this lady is gaga.
Totally cuckoo,
Persona non grata.
So, which someone will sack you?

*- "The Lady is Gaga",
by Augusta Lees*

The Viewdelta Political Series

Brexit's a Trick not a Treat

Brexit's a Musical Trick (not a Treat)
(The Brexit Musical)

Brexit's a Musical Trick CD

I Don't Beg Pardon, I'm Talking Bollocks from
the Rose Garden
(The Covid-19 Musical)

I Don't Beg Pardon CD

It's My Party and I'll Lie if I Want To

 Scan this QR code for more
information:

FOREWORD by MIKE

The absurdities and contradictions of our politics first motivated me in 2016 to highlight them in song. Five years, three books, thousands of online shares, two musical albums and hundreds of online videos later, the material has expanded.

In this book you can find dozens of parody songs, most of which we have recorded for you. You can also find some commentary by Lord Toritori and Mr Curtis Lee-Smugg.

This is my first collaboration with Augusta and it's a real joy to work with someone so quick and witty who uses her wonderful musical talent to such good effect. A real cabaret star. And an eagle-eyed proof-reader! See what you think of our collaborative songs for the "Rejoin EU" movement.

The subject matter is of course serious. I hope you agree with me that there is still a place for humour, to inform and amuse.

To anyone offended, I apologise.

We hope you enjoy reading and singing these pieces, and seeing more than 120 videos of this material – just scan the QR codes, where included, to go directly to a relevant recording.

♪   - Book includes link to a musical recording

♪ - Book includes link to a spoken recording

ACKNOWLEDGMENTS by AUGUSTA

There are always too many to thank when you look back at the help and support given, but thank you first to all my wonderful Twitter friends without whose likes, comments (good and bad!) and retweets gave me an ever-increasing platform, confidence boosts and many laughs to keep creating these parodies. Often ideas were suggested and some found and tinkered with, so where applicable I have tried to namecheck each of those within the songs in the book, apologies to anyone I may have missed.

I would also like to thank the scientific, disability, post viral and Long Covid communities for their early encouragement, particularly on Covid related songs which meant these last two years have felt a little less lonely.

My amazing parents and brother need special mention for their support, particularly through many periods of ill health and putting up with all the years of repetitive piano practice. Also my wonderful piano teacher Maggie MacLennan who always inspired and encouraged.

Final thanks must go to Mike for taking me on this crazy whirlwind journey within a few months of crossing paths. How wonderful to find a new friend and kindred parody spirit.

ORGANISED by SCANDAL

The number of scandals that the Conservative Government managed to sustain simultaneously in 2021-2022 was remarkable.

As well as the Brexit shambles and the ineffective response to Covid, more news emerged about the corrupt contracting for Covid supplies, and the Tories scrambled to change the rules to shield a corrupt lobbyist MP from the consequences of his actions. Meanwhile, more and more information was divulged concerning the illegal parties held in Downing Street.

This book is therefore arranged in thematic chapters, broadly in line with the various scandals unfolding simultaneously before the public's astonished eyes.

Any dates shown are when we wrote the songs, sometimes a few days after the news story.

Where we have adapted a well-known song, the name of the original song is included for reference. Our thanks are due to the brilliant original writers and performers – as well as to the very talented singers who have recorded many of these songs – mostly by Augusta, but Leon Berger, Pat Hart and Carole Williams also feature.

The original lyrics (for each song parodied here) and recordings of it should be available online in most cases.

Please enjoy the humour and write a review!

THE LIZ ATRUSSITIES 2nd EDITION

We had planned to publish the original book during the week Boris Johnson was replaced; then we postponed publication for two weeks after the death of the Queen. But as soon had we published, opportunities flooded in to lampoon Truss, Kwarteng and colleagues.

In response to pleas from fans, following Liz Truss's short but disastrous leadership, we have packed into this new "Plus Truss" edition our observations in poetry and song on her ludicrous leadership.

Seeking to avoid increasing the cost of the book, we have made a few compromises. Much of the "back material" describing our earlier books and music has gone – please look at our website www.viewedelta.com instead. Some of the earlier sketches have been shrunk to a QR code – you can still find the video using the QR code, but the text is no longer included in this second edition.

So we have been able to squeeze in 30 more songs and poems about the Autumn of Atrussities, within two new chapters:
* Our Economy and How They Wrecked It
* More Liz Atrussities and Other Chaos.

We hope you enjoy the result.
Mike and Augusta

- Mike Cashman and Augusta Lees -

It's My Party and I'll Lie If I Want To

Contents

Our Economy and How They Wrecked It 164

Where were we?

In this book there are a few songs from 2020 or
January 2021 where we have previously published the
lyrics, but we have included them here because we
now have recordings you can watch and listen to,
which was not the case initially.

Wherever you see a QR code, scan that with your
phone to go straight to a video.

Our Leaders

Prime Minister of all UK ♪

Inspired by: *Now He Is the Ruler of the Queen's Navy (HMS Pinafore, Gilbert & Sullivan)*

31 December 2020
Mike: An update. Sung by Leon Berger, with Zena Wigram on choruses and Selwyn Tillett on the piano.

When I was a hack, I raised a laugh,
With silly pieces for the Telegraph,
Of bent bananas – what would get a rise.
I wrote those articles though they were lies.
(He wrote those articles though they were lies).
I wrote those articles and earned good pay,
And now I am Prime Minister of all UK.
(He wrote those articles and earned good pay,
And now he is Prime Minister of all UK).

As journalist I cut a dash,
And they made me the Mayor of the London Bash.
I invented buses with a funny quirk,
With a bridge and water cannons that didn't work,
(With a bridge and water cannons that didn't work).
For the bridge and water cannons folk had to pay,
But now I am Prime Minister of all UK.
(For the bridge and water cannons folk had to pay,
But now he is Prime Minister of all UK).

For the Leave campaign I rode a bus
With a slogan on the side that we won't discuss.
Well, I hoped to lose in a glorious way,
But sadly, I won at the end of the day.
(But sadly, he won at the end of the day).
I won that vote, though Theresa May
Was then Prime Minister of all UK
(He won that vote, though Theresa May
Was then Prime Minister of all UK).

I got a majority and now I feel
I can threaten everyone we'll Leave No Deal,
But I know some would view that as a failure,
So, instead I will talk about Australia.
(So, instead he will talk about Australia).
I talked such drivel 'most every day;
You can do that when you're PM of all UK.
(He talks such drivel 'most every day;
You can do that when you're PM of all UK).

The time that I'd like to talk about Leave
Will be afternoon on Christmas Eve.
And so, to make true my Christmas wish,
We'll argue all night then concede on Fish.
(They'll argue all night then concede on Fish).
I'll concede on Fish in the light of day;
You can do that when you're PM of the whole UK.
(He'll concede on Fish in the light of day;
You can do that when you're PM of the whole UK).

Now MPs all whoever you may be,
If you want to rise to the top of the tree,
You can treat the electorate as if they're fools
If you're not constrained by the normal Rules.
(He's not constrained by the normal Rules).
So, don't hold me to anything I'll say,
'Cos I'm Prime Minister of all UK.
(So, don't hold him to anything he'll say,
'Cos He's Prime Minister of all UK).

I Will Survive...Meanwhile at Melania's ♪
Inspired by: *I Will Survive,* Gloria Gaynor

Augusta: Recorded in the early hours of 18th
November 2020 when the result was, finally,
announced that Donald Trump had lost his election
bid for another term in office. Apologies for the dodgy
accent if you watch the video.

At first, I was afraid, I was petrified,
Thinking you would leave the White House and be
back by my side.
And I spent so many nights thinking how you did me
wrong,

And I grew strong.
One day soon, Don will be gone.

For now, you're back,
Your orange face.

I just walked in to find you off the green and, eurgh,
that saggy face.
I should have changed that stupid lock,
Or, maybe signed divorce decree.
If I knew for just one second, you'd be back to bother
me.

Go on now go,
Walk out the door.
Just turn around now,
You fat, racist, sexist, bore.

Weren't you the one,
Who tried to hurt me with your lies,
Each grimy fumble.
You think I'd lay down and die.

No, no, not I, I will survive,
As long I know how to…
(Gestures shh finger to lip)
I know I will survive.
Give me a few years to outlive.
You've got all your stocks to give.
And I'll survive, I will survive.
Hey, hey.

The Donald Went Down to Georgia ♪

Inspired by: *The Devil Went Down to Georgia*
5 January 2021

Mike: NB When the Donald went down to Georgia it was not surprising that the idea of a parody was not unique to me. So, massive respect also to Aaron Gage; on the same day that I composed and published these lyrics, he composed a "Donald Went Down to Georgia" song and - this is where the massive respect comes - he then played all the instruments, mixed a video with him playing all the instruments and singing, and you can see that on YouTube too. By the time his video came out my lyrics were already published - the timelines show that we were working independently. Aaron Gage's video is great, and I hope that you enjoy this one too – sung on the video by Pat Hart.

The Donald went down to Georgia.
He was lookin' for some votes to steal.
He was in a bind,
'Cause he was way behind,
And he was willin' to make a deal.

When he came across this official
Sitting on a vote pile and playin' it straight,
And the Donald played all on a telephone call,
And said, "Man, I want your State".

"I guess you didn't know it,
But I can fiddle things too,

And if you'd care to take a dare,
I'll make a deal with you.

Now you'll do a pretty good fiddle, hey,
But give the Donald his due.
I'll bet a fiddle of gold
Against your soul
Twelve thousand votes from you".

The man said, "Raffensperger's
My name, and I won't sin.
This is worst yet, you're gonna regret,
This call will be called in".

Brad Raffensperger you won't try that fiddle hard,
'Cause Hell's broke loose in Georgia,
And the Donald deals the cards.
And if you win, you'll see
That your true story will be told.
But if you lose, the Donald gets your soul.

The Donald opened up his case,
And he said, "I'll start this show."
Bad words flew from his evil lips,
As he threatened him, you know.

And he said he'd notify a crime,
Put Raffen on the floor,
And the band of his supporters

Made threats of civil war.

When the Donald finished,
Raffen said, "Well, you've had your say, ol' son,
But sit down in that chair right there,
And let me show you how it's done."

"Fix on the ballots", run boys, run.
The Donald's in the House of the Washington.
Tweets full of nonsense, supersized fries.
Cotton-pickin' voters spot your lies".

The Donald bowed his head,
He should know that he's been beat.
And it's time to lose that fiddle.
Joe Biden needs his seat.

Raffen said, "Donald, just don't come back,
And don't you try again.
I done told you once, you son of a bitch,
You're the worst that's ever been."

"Fix on the ballots", run boys, run.
The Donald's in the House of the Washington.
Tweets full of nonsense, supersized fries.
Cotton-pickin voters spot your lies".

When We Break Up (Oyster Snack) ♪

Inspired by: *I Would Walk 500 Miles*
January 2021

Mike: I originally wrote this song July 2020 after Boris Johnson made a pointless trip to Scotland to be photographed with some fishermen's catch in Orkney and at an RAF base in Lossiemouth. Pat Hart recorded this, and I planned to release a video using that recording the next time that Boris Johnson made a significant visit to Scotland. In fact, his most significant visits were 2021(continued the visit despite a member of staff testing positive for Covid) and 2022 (to Balmoral to see the Queen to resign).
But here for you is the video now. Scan that QR code!
Postscript: RAF Lossiemouth also supplied the RAF fighter jet for Johnson's post-resignation joyride.

When we break up, well I know I'm gonna be,
I'm gonna be the man who builds the SNP.
When I get out, well I know I'm gonna be,
I'm gonna be the man who trashed things with EC.

If I don't plan, well I know I'm gonna be,
I'm gonna be the man who won't plan next to you.
And if I mess up, yes I know I'm gonna be,
I'm gonna be the man who's messing next to you.

But I would fly 500 miles, and I would fly 500 back,
Just to be the man who flies a thousand miles
To grab an oyster snack.

When I'm bluffing, yes I know I'm gonna be,
I'm gonna be the man who's bluffing next for you.
And when the millions, comes in for the loans I do,
I'll won't pass so many pennies on to you.

When I broadcast (when I broadcast),
Well, I know I'm gonna be,
I'm gonna be the man who broadcasts worse than you.
Easing lockdown (easing lockdown),
Well, I know I'm gonna be,
I'll be easing lockdown. which I shouldn't do.

But I would fly 500 miles, and I would fly 500 back,
Just to be the man who flies a thousand miles
To grab an oyster snack.

Hi and bye bye (Hi and bye bye),
Hi and bye bye (Hi and bye bye),
Hi and bye bye fiddle a fiddle a fiddle a bye,
Lie ba die die (lie ba die die).
Lie ba die die (lie ba die die),
Lie ba die die fiddle a fiddle a fiddle a bye.

When I'm lonely, well I think that we will see
Who'll gonna be the ones who quickly fly here too.
And when they're coming, they'll build up the SNP.
They're going to fly around and blindly insult you.

When they go out (when they go out),
Well you know they're gonna be,
They're going to be within the Baxter's, that's so true.
And when they're talking (when they're talking),
Well, I know they're gonna be,
They're going to be the ones who will embarrass you.
They're going to be the ones who will embarrass you.

But I would fly 500 miles, and I would fly 500 back,
Just to be the man who flies a thousand miles
To grab an oyster snack.

Hi and bye bye (Hi and bye bye),
Hi and bye bye (Hi and bye bye),
Hi and bye bye fiddle a fiddle a fiddle a bye,
Lie ba die die (lie ba die die),
Lie ba die die (lie ba die die),
Lie ba die die fiddle a fiddle a fiddle a bye.
Hi and bye bye (Hi and bye bye),
Hi and bye bye (Hi and bye bye),
Hi and bye bye fiddle a fiddle a fiddle a bye.
Lie ba die die (lie ba die die),
Lie ba die die (lie ba die die),
Lie ba die die fiddle a fiddle a fiddle a bye.

But I would fly 500 miles, and I would fly 500 back,
Just to be the man who flies a thousand miles
To grab an oyster snack.
(Supporters: Hear hear, hear hear)

Time Is Running Out ♪

Inspired by: *Time Is Running Out,* Muse
25 January 2022
Augusta: It was extraordinary that he clung on for so many months more.

You see him drowning, asphyxiated,
As more MPs rebel, egos deflated.
He's inexcusable, but near eviction,
He tries to lay the blame, gets crucifixion.

Who will be the death (political) of him?
It's time to see who'll sink or swim.

Will Sue Gray acquit?
Won't let her bury it.
Oh look delays have hit, (how convenient)
And now The Met's at it.

But his time is running out,
P45s about.
Can't hide under the ground, (PMQs?)
Will he be scheming now?

How did it come to this?
Blackmail and lies, yeah, yeah, yeah, yeah.
Racist replies, yeah, yeah, yeah, yeah.

Covid and crimes, yeah, they don't care.

Yeah, this has sucked the life out of us,
Covid and Brexit,
Bad news won't bury it,
The truths unravel it,
One more Good Law Project.

His time is running out,
No friends to fight it out,
Dead cats are underground,
Is there redeeming now?
How did it come to this?

Blackmail and lies, yeah, yeah, yeah, yeah.
Throw in some spies, yeah, yeah, yeah, yeah.
Who cares who dies, yeah, we despair.
(Tick, tock)

Prime Minister's Voicemail ≑

Oh, hello there.
This is the Prime Minister's voicemail.
That's still me at the moment, Boris
Johnson.
At any rate it's still me unless Dom spills any more
beans.
Enter your donation to the Tories and press hash.

This should be a number of six digits or more.
If you have donated before, you should still donate again.
Spero tibi magnus valde
That's Latin for,
I hope yours is a very big one. (Chuckles)
Then key 1 for favourable tax treatment,
2 for crony contracts,
3 for legislative favours,
4 if you wish to be appointed to a role
for which you are not competent.
5 to break international law.
6 if you'd like to hire a spiffing room
we spaffed 2.6 million roubles on,
or 7 if you are offering private technology lessons.
(chuckles)
But if you want a Public Inquiry
Et quia modo sibilus
and that is Latin for "You can whistle for it now".
If you wish to ask about Welsh national vegetables,
we never comment on leeks unless we feel like it.
If you are Dominic Cummings,
you can not have your old job back,
and I sincerely hope that your phone explodes.
Have a jolly good day the rest of you,
and remember face, place, space, case, pace, or something.
Pip pip.

Another Aide Bites the Dust ♪

Inspired by: *Another One Bites The Dust,* Queen

Augusta: Recorded 14th November 2020.
A flurry of aides left Downing Street this week,
culminating in the biggest news of all - Dominic
Cummings was sacked, six months after the Rose
Garden 'no regrets' speech.

Another aide bites the dust.
Dom's gotta go catch the bus.
And another one gone, another gone,
Another one bites the dust.
Hey! Can you take Boris too?
Another one bites the dust.

Rishi, Rishi, Rishi, Rishi ♪

Inspired by: *Ruby,* Kaiser Chiefs

Augusta: It was revealed that £4.3 billion pounds
would be written off from fraudulent Covid loans. But
our National Insurance rise was going to go ahead,
despite Conservative manifesto pledges to the
contrary. This all seemed perfectly sensible from the
Chancellor of the Exchequer Rishi Sunak.
30th January 2022.

Rishi, Rishi, Rishi, Rishi,
Where did £4 billion go?
Well do ya, do ya, do ya,
Think tax payers should know?
Know what you're doing, doing to me?
My pay now takes the hit.
Well Rishi, Rishi, Rishi, Rishi,
Your NI rise is sh...
(Shocking really isn't it?)

How Does He Survive? ♪

Inspired by: *I Will Survive,* Gloria Gaynor, suggested by Shoshana D.

Augusta: After another flurry of aides jumped ship, Guto Harri was one of the more prominent replacements. This was recorded February 8th 2022, after a bizarre exchange was released to the press as Guto apparently saluted Boris as he 'reported to duty', and Boris sang I Will Survive at him, followed by a little duet. Every satirist in the country without warning became redundant.

A burst of new aides, and we're petrified.
Thinking you might never leave your post and stand aside. (Democracy)
We've spent so many nights, thinking soon you must be gone.

But we were wrong.
Somehow still you scrape along.
(Well he's not a complete clown!)*

Knives in your back,
Each new disgrace,
How much more of this, can we all take?
His lying, smirking face.
We should have known he likes to mock,
From women to minorities.
But this Starmer jab on top of that, it's just
cowardly.**

Go on, now go! (Please)
Walk out the door.
No more U-turns now.
We can't take this anymore.

Johnson's the one who hurts this country with his lies.
Each time he's rumbled.
Does anybody trust this guy?

Oh no, not I.
Yet he survives. (How?)
As long as there's some Russian love, he keeps his
career alive.
We've got all our lives to live,
It's not forever (God) forbid,
So I'll survive. And you'll survive.
(But he won't indefinitely)

Hey. Hey.

*'Boris Johnson is 'not a complete clown' one of Guto Harri's first remarks as new press chief. Comforting.

**Boris Johnson still refused to correct the record after the false accusation that Keir Starmer had failed to investigate Jimmy Saville as part of his job as Director of Public Prosecutions.

You Shalt Have a Hissy ♪

Inspired by: *When the Boat Comes In Augusta: Turns out that Rishi Sunak was also pictured at these parties. 10th February 2022.*

Something's looking fishy,
If your name is Rishi,
And your little wishy's,
Dobbing Boris in.

You shalt have a hissy,
If there's Christmas piccies,
Of your lockdown drinkies,
Champagne and quizzing.

Soon goes Big Doggy,
Can he take Moggy?
Nadine is groggy,
Now let's watch the spin.

Carrie's had a paddy,
Wants a new big daddy.
We shall all be gladdy,
When they're in the bin.

Edward Leigh ♪
Inspired by: *Let It Be*, The Beatles

Augusta: This was a response to Sir Edward Leigh's words at the start of the Ukrainian war crisis, in a speech to the House of Commons on the 1st March. He said that in Lincolnshire "we've done our bit with migration from Eastern Europe". When there was a tiny semblance of unity with the outpouring of support from all political sides, this man stood out. It took a couple of days for my rage to suitably percolate before I recorded this on 3rd March 2022.

When we find ourselves in times of trouble,
A Gainsborough MP's on TV.
Speaks his words of wisdom,
Edward Leigh (Sir Edward).

And in this hour of darkness,
He is standing right in front of me,
Vomits his words of wisdom,
A travesty.
(Seriously who is he?)

Gouty flea, Edward Leigh,
Refugees? 'No, not for me'.
He thinks he is the victim,
So cowardly.

Racist spree, from Edward Leigh,
Gammon plea, said with glee.
Putrefied words of dribble,
You don't speak for me.

Dillie Keane particularly liked "Putrefied words of dribble".

Fancy Dress Liz Truss ♪

Inspired by: *That Don't Impress Me Much,* Shania Twain

Augusta: Led by Boris Johnson, the Conservative Government seemed to spend more time dressing up than doing any work, Johnson had the biggest dressing up box but Liz Truss was a close second. 5th March 2022.

I've known a few guys who like to play the part,
(Boris)
She's got being vain down to an art.

Each picture's more heinous,
Drives us up the wall.
A narcissistic criminal,
Does she work at all?

Oh-oh costumes don't make you special.
Oh-oh she's playing someone else.
(Again... – Ooh, extra in Dr Zhivago?)

It's fancy-dress Liz Truss. (Where are my flags?)
She's got no brains,
And she's out of touch.
Now don't get me wrong,
Wannabe Thatcherite,
And that don't keep me calm in the middle of the night.

(How is she Foreign Secretary?)*
We're not impressed Liz Truss.

Mike: The Liz Truss "Thatcher Tribute Act" photo-shoots were a clear indication of her plan to bid for the leadership after Johnson was dispatched. – as, of course, was Rishi Sunak's registration of his website.
*Update at time of publication. How is she Prime Minister?

Gavin's Hard Work ♪

Inspired by: *A Hard Day's Night,* The Beatles

Augusta: 3rd March 2022 it was announced Gavin Williamson was to be given a knighthood, even though he'd been sacked from the cabinet. Twice. And he generally displayed world beating incompetence in a crowd of Conservative contenders. He lost his position in Theresa May's government after an inquiry about leaking information, and then he oversaw various education debacles during the pandemic under Johnson which, also led to his dismissal. F for effort and achievement.

So Gavin's hard work comes right,
Despite being twice sacked from his job.
(Happens to us all)
It's not hard to make him a knight,
He's got the dirt all catalogued.

Failing kids is so cool,
The leaks weren't that criminal.
So knighthood feels all right.

Hey Rishi ♪

Inspired by: *Hey Mickey*, Toni Basil, suggested and brainstormed with Shuaib Khan

Augusta: After the budget statement was released which included the whole five pence fuel duty cut, (which only meant that the garages pushed up prices following the announcement), there was no surprise that the millionaire chancellor Rishi Sunak was all over the news. Highlights included him being unable to use contactless payment in a service station and admitting to having 5 different types of bread in his house for each family member. Not quite the breadline I was referring to when I sang on 25th March 2022.

Hey Rishi, we're not fine, we're not fine on the breadline,
Hey Rishi! Richie Rishi.
Hey Rishi, please resign, all your mates got loans, not mine.
Hey Rishi, something's fishy?

The millionaire is tight as we barely scrape along.
You say the statements right,
But we know you've got it wrong.
Why can't you see our plight?
Why can't I heat my home Rishi?
(Imagine heating 12 of them?!)

You say you'll help our bills,

It always means you won't.
His face gives me the chills,
(Tax the rich, no you don't)
Every shop's a thrill, will I need a loan?
(At least I know how to use a checkout)

Oh Rishi, what a pity,
You don't understand.
You tear us all apart,
When you don't give us a hand.

Oh Rishi, looking shifty,
Saville Row conman.
It's guys like you Rishi.
(Don't have a clue)

Look at fuel duty, 5 pennies?!
What a sure start Rishi!
(Oops don't mention Sure Start, already cut that) *

** Sure Start Centres were designed to help improve
health and education of early years children,
particularly in deprived areas. Since 2010 (I wonder
what happened that year), funding has been
drastically cut resulting in 500 sites closing by 2019.
The IFS (Institute for Fiscal Studies) research found
the centres had provided clear improvement in
children's health and wellbeing, particularly when
looking at hospital admissions in under 11s.*

- Mike Cashman and Augusta Lees -

Our Pandemic

Twelve Days of Lockdown ♪

Inspired by: *Twelve Days of Christmas*
Augusta: This was my first publicly shared parody,
which I wrote just before the second lockdown in
November 2020, I posted onto Facebook the day new
restrictions came into effect 5th November 2020.
Thank you to Conor Browne for the late-night
brainstorming.

On the first day of lockdown my true
love gave to me:
A proper set of PPE.

On the second day of lockdown my true
love gave to me:
2 latex gloves,
And a proper set of PPE.

On the third day of lockdown my true love gave to me:
3 deep cleans,
2 latex gloves and a proper set of PPE.

On the 4th day of lockdown my true love gave to me:
4 Nightingales,
3 deep cleans, 2 latex gloves and a proper set of PPE.

On the 5th day of lockdown my true love gave to me:
Dexamethasone.

4 Nightingales, 3 deep cleans, 2 latex gloves and a
proper set of PPE.

On the 6th day of lockdown my true love gave to me:
6 ventilators.
Click and Collect.
4 Nightingales, 3 deep cleans, 2 latex gloves and a
proper set of PPE.

On the 7th day of lockdown my true love gave to me:
7 fogged up visors, 6 ventilators,
Jonathan Van-Tam.
4 Nightingales, 3 deep cleans, 2 latex gloves and a
proper set of PPE.

On the 8th day of lockdown my true love gave to me:
8 glaring loopholes, 7 fogged up visors, 6 ventilators,
Barnard Castle.
4 Nightingales, 3 deep cleans, 2 latex gloves and a
proper set of PPE.

On the 9th day of lockdown my true love gave to me:
9 zoom codes waiting, 8 glaring loopholes, 7 fogged
up visors, 6 ventilators,
Can you hear me now?!
4 Nightingales, 3 deep cleans, 2 latex gloves and a
proper set of PPE.

On the 10th day of lockdown my true love gave to me:
10 days isolation, 9 zoom codes waiting, 8 glaring
loopholes, 7 fogged up visors, 6 ventilators,
I can't smell a thing?!

4 Nightingales, 3 deep cleans, 2 latex gloves and a proper set of PPE.

On the 11th day of lockdown my true love gave to me:
11 anti-maskers, 10 days isolation, 9 zoom codes waiting, 8 glaring loopholes, 7 fogged up visors, 6 ventilators,
Mask goes ON your nose *.
4 Nightingales, 3 deep cleans, 2 latex gloves and a proper set of PPE.

On the 12th day of lockdown my true love gave to me:
(Wish me luck...) **
12 contact tracers, 11 anti-maskers, 10 days isolation, 9 zoom codes waiting, 8 glaring loopholes, 7 fogged up visors, 6 ventilators,
PLEASE STAY AT HOME!
4 Nightingales, 3 deep cleans, 2 latex gloves and a proper set of PPE.
Merry Lockdown!

In the video I sing please wear your mask.
**You have no idea how many takes this took for a nearly 5 min video. Never again. And why did I decide to do 3 octave leaps in the right hand in the final verse?!*

Vaccine ♪

Inspired by: *Jolene*, Dolly Parton
Augusta: Recorded 13 November 2020, after the news that Pfizer's vaccine was shown to be more than 90% effective in preventing Covid-19. I remember the relief I felt then and the hope that we were nearing the end. How wrong can you be, looking at you Delta variant.

Vaccine, Vaccine, Vaccine, Vaccine.
I'm begging of you please work if you can.
Vaccine, Vaccine, Vaccine, Vaccine.
Please take us back before it all began.

Your science is beyond compare,
mRNA it don't play fair.
The mink mutated strain was unforeseen.
I talk about you in my sleep,
And there's nothing I can do to keep,
From crying when I hear Covid-19.
And I can hardly understand,
How much this virus wrecked our plans,
I just want to hold those close to me.

Vaccine, Vaccine, Vaccine, Vaccine.
I'm begging of you please work if you can.
Vaccine, Vaccine, Vaccine, Vaccine.
Please take us back before it all began.*
Vaccine.
* I sing please take us back to where we all began. A bit philosophical.

This Christmas ♪

Inspired by: *Last Christmas,* George Michael, with a
Jingle Bell ending in recording.

*Augusta: Written 22 December 2020 after Boris
Johnson repeatedly said no additional restrictions
would come into place, but a huge part of the country
was put into Tier 4 meaning they could not socialise
outside of their household or bubble. The rest of the
country was in Tier 3 meaning they could only visit on
Christmas Day rather than the original 5-day rule.*

This Christmas, we might be apart,
Boris had his say, then took it away.
This year, we might still be in tiers,
But somehow we'll make it special.

This Christmas, we might be apart,
But we'll find a way, to make it a day.
This year, we might be stuck in tears.
But I know we can make it special, special.*

Once infected, twice shy.
I kept my distance, but thousands did not comply.

Tell me baby, do you recognise me?
Well, it's been such a year, it wouldn't surprise me.

Merry Christmas, I wrapped it up and sent it,
With a note saying, I love you I meant it.
Now the posties working nights again,
Parcels so high, they don't know where to begin.

This Christmas we might be apart,
But at home we stay, to keep Covid at bay.
Next year, we might get the all clear.
And God it will feel so special.

Merry Christmas.
I sang repeat of somehow we'll make it special.

Where's Chris Whitty? ♪

Inspired by: *I Feel Pretty,* Leonard Bernstein

*Augusta: Cases, hospitalisations and deaths were
rising fast with another Covid-19 wave but there was
barely a mention from the Government, and the Chief
Medical Officer Professor Whitty was notably absent.
"Where's Wally"- style memes abounded on Twitter.
Professor Jonathan Van Tam who had often spoken
out when nobody else would, had recently resigned as
Deputy Chief Medical Officer.*

Where's Chris Whitty?
Search the city?
It's a pity, 'cause Whitty could say,
Yeah, it's shitty (language Chris) but
the virus has not gone away.
(I miss Van Tam)

Oh Shingles, Shingles ♪

Inspired by: *Baby One More Time,* Britney Spears
March 2021

*Augusta: More of a personal one. Mid lockdown
number three, to add insult to injury, in a world
dominated by viruses, my body decided to reactivate
the chicken pox virus and give me shingles. When the
pain had subsided enough, I was able to record this,
although the grimaces on the video were real.*

Oh shingles, shingles,
How was I supposed to know?
That something wasn't right here.

Oh shingles, shingles,
I shouldn't have let you grow.
And now you're on my side, yeah.

Show me, says the Dr, to me,
Tell me maybe, 'cause I need to know, ow,
What's the cause?

My rashiness is killing me. (A bit dramatic)
I must confess I need relief. (Need relief)
When I'm stuck with you, I lose my mind.
I draw the line,
Don't hit me shingles in spring time.

Should He Stay, or Should He Go? ♪
Inspired by: *Should I Stay or Should I Go?* The Clash

 Augusta: This song was calling for Boris Johnson to consider his position as Prime Minister, particularly due to the inept handling of the pandemic. May 27th 2021.

Boris you gotta let us know,
Should you stay or should you go?
If you say that things are fine.
Who'll get the blame and then resign? (Hancock)*
Bolton, Bedford and Hounslow,
Should they stay or should they go. (Anywhere?)**

You're always "Please, please, please,
Why are the doctors on their knees?"
Which SAGE member will first crack?
It's time to blunder and backtrack. (Again)
Well, come on and let us know,
Which data next will you forgo?

Just on holiday we go now.
Is it amber, green or red now?
If you go there will be trouble.
Yes, the case rates here will double.
So come on and let us know...

How many chances can you blow?

- Mike Cashman and Augusta Lees -

You must listen to this piece for nothing else other than my very musical elbow.

* This was a few months before Hancock did indeed become the next sacrificial lamb.
** A very odd moment of the pandemic when the government website was updated to essentially put these towns and some others with very high incidences of Covid into local lockdowns suggesting they don't leave the area. However, they failed to contact the relevant local authorities or public.

Mad World ♪

Inspired by: *Mad World*, the Gary Jules cover

Augusta: A more sober song to mark the end of all protective measures against Covid-19 in the UK 24th February 2022. Clinically Vulnerable (CV) and Clinically Extremely Vulnerable (CEV) families were thrown to the wolves. Coinciding with the Russian invasion of Ukraine it was a very mad and sad world that day.

All around me are so many cases,
Unsafe places, unmasked faces.
Bright and early for the daily races,
But I'm going nowhere, going nowhere.

CV tears are filling up their glasses,
No expression, no connection.
Hide your head, don't want to see our sorrow.

No tomorrow, no tomorrow.

And I find it kind of funny,
Find it kind of sad.
Our dreams are slowly dying,
Who knew freedom felt so bad.
The experts all will tell you,
Public finds it hard to take.
So people run in circles,

It's a very, very, mad world.
Sad world.

Boris Bonka and the Variant factory
A story that is not for children

Now, if there are any children here then this story is not for you, but it's all about a man called Boris Bonka who had a factory for making variants - Boris Bonka's variant factory, or some people just called it the Bonka's variant factory.

Boris Bonka had put Ivor Grandcock in charge of the variant factory, which tended to be quite busy during a pandemic, but Boris Bonka's previous personal assistant and main operative. Mr. Long Shortcomings had told everyone that Boris Bonka knew that Ivor Grandcock was useless at the job. Ivor Grandcock had

 managed to make one variant, but Boris Bonka was still not satisfied.

Scan the QR code to hear more

I'm B16, B1617 ♪

Inspired by: *I Am 16, Going On 17*
May 2021
Mike: I spoke on BBC Radio 4 "Any Answers" to make the same points as are made in the song and was described by the presenter Anita Anand as a "meaty first caller" Sung on this video by Pat Hart.

Just wait, little bug, as you have the floor
Where you've got a free pass now.
You rate, little bug, an infection score,
So you can kick their R's now,
-   Their R's now.

I'm B16, B16 17,
My numbers not yet high.
For you I'm heading, community spreading,
Starting to multiply.
More than a ripple, weekly I'll triple,
Everyone must take care.
Vaccinate all, was Blackburn's clear call,
But London said "Don't you dare".

Mod'rately unprepared are they
To face this spreading strain.
Are people not so scared today
Don't want Lock Down again?

You'll need tactics faster and wiser
Dealing with my outbreaks;
Surge vaccinate before it's too late -

A million shots what it takes.

You're B16, B16 17,
Your numbers could be high.
Each week infect more, we should protect more,
Before you multiply.
We mustn't slumber, or else the number
Could rocket through the roof.
Care is essential, growth exponential
Might happen, that's the truth.
Mod'rately unprepared are we
To face this spreading strain.
Are people not so scared today
Don't want Lock Down again?

We'll need someone older and wiser,
Witnesses in their turn.
As folk get fiery,
Hold an Inquiry,
Lessons we need to learn.

Don't Cry for Them Matt and Gina ♪

Inspired by: *Don't Cry For Me Argentina,* Lloyd-Webber and Rice

Augusta: Matt Hancock finally got the boot, and it wasn't because of his woeful overseeing of the pandemic as Heath Secretary and thousands of preventable deaths. No, he had an *affair and someone leaked footage of him in his office kissing his aide Gina Coladangelo, which made the public angry enough (even after Johnson accepted his apology and considered the matter closed) to force him to resign from the cabinet (not as an MP) on 26th June 2021.*
This was recorded in the early hours of 27th June.

You're all so sleazy, you'll never change.
Don't explain how you copped a feel,
A camera above, caught your hand on her bum.

It all got steamy, and I can't unsee, the aide that you screw.
But now you're dressed up to resign, your ex is a lesson for you.*

Don't snog at work Matt and Gina, the truth is your conscience left you.
Pandemic wild days, just one mad instance.
A broken promise, from lack of distance.

How could you let it happen, are you estranged?
From your family, your wife, how do they feel?
Looking out of the window,
You're front page of The Sun.
Who will succeed him?
A health secretary who might have a clue.
With cases suppressed after all.
But, I don't expect much, do you?

Don't cry for them Matt and Gina, the truth is your ethics left you.
Pandemic wild days, a mad existence,
We all want solace, but we kept our distance...
* Augusta: Still my most proud parody lyric from the original "At sixes and sevens".

We Don't Have No Mitigations ♪

Inspired by: *We Don't Need No Education,* Pink Floyd

Augusta: A song recorded 2nd November 2021 in response to JCVI (Joint Committee for Vaccines and Immunisation) deciding not to vaccinate 'healthy' children over 12, despite overwhelming evidence that it would protect them. This was at a point where child hospitalisations and deaths were rising faster than at any other time in the pandemic because of the more transmissible, and more likely to affect children more seriously, Delta variant. The effect of 'freedom' day in July meant there were no mitigations in school or anywhere else so case rates sky rocketed.

At the time over 100 children had died, thousands had been hospitalised and 77k kids had Long Covid. Countries around the world, in Europe and USA had adopted vaccines months before and had gone some way to protect children from unnecessary infection. Here not so much. British exceptionalism at its finest.

We don't have no mitigations,
JCVI lost control,
Cataclysms in the classroom,
Tories think it's overblown.
Hey teachers, parents,
Do you feel alone?
All in all, it's just another brick in the wall.
Would they care if you're another heart on the wall?

Covid's in the Air ♪

Inspired by: *Walking in the Air, (The Snowman),* Howard Blake

Augusta: These parodies were born from being a medically vulnerable musician unable, initially to do any of my normal performing due to lockdowns, and latterly because the government and the rest of the world fail, even by this first publication date, to get control of the pandemic. Recorded 20th December 2021 this was another Christmas and winter dominated by Covid-19 for those keeping up with the science. Despite boosters the new vaccine-evading variant Omicron hit the UK in November.

Covid's in the air,
It's floating all around your rooms,
The people far below sleep walk into its plumes.
(How about some mitigations in school, seeing as it's airborne?)

 My mask is very tight,
I'm really hoping yours is too.
(FFP2? Good choice)
Still finding there are some who say
it's just the flu. (Déjà vu)

People gaze open mouthed, (where's your mask?)
Taken by surprise,
Nobody in the know believes their eyes.
*(Apart from actually quite a lot of people, including
the ones above [a group of leading scientists tagged
on Twitter], who have repeatedly said that, no-one is
safe until we're all safe, and vaccine inequity, plus
hesitancy, and just letting a novel virus rip through
populations with quite a lot of immuno-suppressed
people may lead to a vaccine evading variant..)*

Omicron is here,
I'm watching cases go sky high. (Don't cry, don't cry)
You know what's coming next,
So how many will comply?*
(Merry Covid Christmas and a Happy New Wave)

**Augusta: "How many more will die?" was the
original ending but even I found it too tragic to sing.*

When the Covgiants Came ⚏

Mike: A tale for teaching children
Critical Thinking
(My grandchildren love this).
This one is a spoken story only – it has
never been written down, so you have
to scan the QR code to hear it.

Listen to how the dwarves and elves and goblins each
had their own ways of trying to battle with the
incoming Covgiants, which were not proving effective,
until the Wise Old Wizard said to them "What do you
really want?" and helped them to work together in
order to achieve their desired outcome.

Come Fly Mask Free ♪

Inspired by: *Come Fly With Me,* Frank Sinatra, with
suggestion by @its_airborne
16th March 2022

Augusta: British Airways announced that it was
removing mask mandates on its flights as did a
number of other airlines. Funny how shortly
afterwards so many became short staffed and flights
were cancelled. Turns out when Covid-19 is airborne
planes are not.

Come fly mask free,
Might die, but that's OK!
(Come on, live a little, or not)

Your brain may lose function worse than booze,
Clots and scars in your airway.
(Totally normal)
Sequalae for free, standby, don't fly BA.
(Or first-class upgrade? Complimentary FFP3)

Hey, Hey ♪

Inspired by: *The Monkees Theme Song*

Augusta: Recorded on the day the WHO (World Health Organisation) declared the Monkey Pox outbreak a Public Health Emergency of International Concern (PHEIC) with rapidly rising cases across the globe, 23rd July 2022.

 Here they come,
Scratching down the street, *
They get the funniest looks from,
Everyone they meet.
Hey, hey they got Monkey…Pox.

* Originally sang "itching" before I realised "scratching" scanned better.

Their Corruption

With No Tender ♪

Inspired by: *Love Me Tender*

November 2020

Mike: Many of these songs are written within a day or two of the relevant events. This one is an exception. I kept a folder of relevant stories, meaning to work them all into a song. By the time I came to write it I realised that the song would be impossibly long if all the cases were included – and so the lyrics include a selection. If you want to know more about the subject of this song, the best way to get an up-to-date briefing is probably to search online for "The Good Law Project" and their challenge of the contract awards by judicial review. The extent of crony contracting became apparent late in 2020 with a report from the National Audit Office.

In this video, I introduce the song, sung by Carole Williams, which is followed by a sketch which later was developed into a Lord Toritori video.

With no tender, with no checks,
Funding still extends.
Lord knows who is favoured next;
Contracts to their friends.

With no tender, PPE,
That is to Pestfix,
Allocated carefully,
By whose arse he licks.

Millions for a crucial mask.
Have the spec they read?
Sadly they forgot to ask,
Fasten round your head?

Billions wasted on duff kit.
Profits still are banked.
Those who left us in the shit -
Seemingly they're ranked.

What's Ayanda's competence?
Set up yesterday;
Let's forget Due Diligence,
In a rush to pay.

Gove's directing this shit-storm -
"Standing have you none" -
(How he tried to block Jo Maugham
Hiding what they've done).

But to court our heroes go,
As the stakes are upped,
Now Good Law Project can show
How this was corrupt.

With no tender, with no skill,
Corruption we have seen,
Leaving UK much more ill;
Now please buy vaccine.

PPE Procurements – Lord Toritori's Call

LORD TORITORI *(on the phone)*:

Yes, yes.

It's all right, Roland.

A little private spot.

Yeah, nobody can hear us here.

Oh, yes.

You heard about the procurements in
the papers.

Yes, I got the whole thing direct from Squiffy.

So, straight from the donkey's tongue bone
as they don't say in Thessalonica.

Yes. No, no, well perfectly straightforward.

Squiffy and Corker, you see,

they went to school with Vector.

Now, Vector was at Oxford

with you-know-who from the Cabinet.

Yes, they were in some sort of club together.

And now Squiffy and Corker got this company set up.

All totally legit, Companies House and everything.

The office was Squiffy's garage. Yes.

Yes, his wife was a director, as well.

So, the NHS needed literally millions of these masks.

Squiffy got a whiff of who made something like that
in China, Vector put in a good word for him,

and it was all fast-tracked, you see?

Well after all, if you can't make a few million profit
when your great chum is working in 10 Downing
Street, when can you?

Yes, I know. No.

Well, yes, that wasn't really Squiffy's fault.

He had never done anything like that before.

He didn't know the masks had to go around their heads.

No. Check the specs, somebody said.

I thought the Cummings Man was supposed to be doing that in Barnard Castle. *(laughs)*

Yes, that was Corky's joke. *(laughs)*

No, I'm just pulling your plonker, old chap.

Not really. Yes, he checks the specs now.

Yes, but it's not in his garage any more, no.

Because, with the profit, Squiffy was able to buy a rather splendid mansion in the Cotswolds!

Yes.

Yes, that's right.

The first lot, the ones they couldn't use, yes.

But it's OK, because young Rishi Sunak is printing all the money that they need.

So it was no problem, really.

Yeah, so I think they shipped them into Grimsby and nobody knows where they went after that, they've lost them. But they can't use them anyway, so it's not a problem.

Oh, yes, yes!

They call themselves the Good Law Project.

They were led by this oik called Jolyon Maugham.

Yes.

But you-know-who got their measure.

So, what he said was they "Had no Standing".

Now that's lawyer-speak for "None of your damn business". *(laughs)*

Yes, so what they said was it's only the competing firms would be entitled to raise any Judicial Review.

Yes, and here is the best bit, Roland.

Then they tell the competing firms not to make any fuss 'cause if so, they wouldn't get any more damn business.
Yes. But even that, they still came on and there's another trick up their sleeve. So, wait for this one.
So this "Good Law Project" said they should have published the billets-douxs about the contracts, which is all little kerfuffle about nothing.
Since the business was all done by then.
Anyway, they said they ought to publish them.
So, what they did, what you-know-who organised was put every Silk you could imagine onto the attendance sheet.
Yes, yes, him. Yes, yes, so, him, too.
Yeah, Uncle Silk Cobley and all.
So they ran up a bill of 207,000 quid for a one day hearing!
And the point about that is scare the other lot off you see. Yes, rack the costs up, and then the others will be a bit frightened, and I should think they'll go away.
Yes. Oh, hold on, Roland. Hell's bloody pyjamas!
I think Roderick's left his phone recording here.
Yes, I'll have to get back to you.
That was for later. What do you do with this?
Go away. I think it's still recording. Simpkins, Simpkins. I think there's a bloody film on this Ifun.
Do you know how to redact it?
Take the bloody thing off.
I don't want to be appearing with this phone call on Tubular You.
I don't know why Roderick left it on the table.
How do you turn it off, anyway? Oh, okay. Yes.

Once More Unto the Lobbies

Inspired by: *Once More Unto the Breach, Dear Friends, Once More*, from Henry V

Once more unto the lobbies, dear friends, once more,
Or close up amendments with our Tory votes.
At work there is nothing so becomes a man
As acquiescence and a bag of notes.

But when the commissioner blows the whistle,
Then recognise the action of the whips.
Close ranks, protect the wrongdoer in our midst,
And let no word of censure pass our lips.

Do not take criticism on the floor,
The opposition we will treat as nought,
Proceed unconstitutionally - no law
Will e'er inhibit us - unless we're caught
In headlines critical in Daily Mail,
If they declare their righteous and just rage;
For lacking their support we'd surely fail,
If we're called sleazebags on that Mail front page.

Twist T and V's the turn we then must make,
For U-turn if you want to flee the lash
Of those who scorn us as we eat the cake,
And have it with the honours and the cash.
So is it time to relegate PM?
Is his time served, the scapegoat now to shoo?
We'll find another figurehead pro tem.
Don't think that we will ever think of you.

Twelve Days of Tories

Inspired by: *Twelve Days of Christmas*
*Mike: Augusta and I independently chose to parody
this song in different ways.*

On the first day of Tories the PM gave to me
Restrictions from which Tories all are free.

On the 2nd day of Tories the PM gave to me
Two corrupt appointments,
And restrictions from which Tories all are free.

On the 3rd day of Tories the PM gave to me
Three illegal favours, Two corrupt appointments,
And restrictions from which Tories all are free.

.. and so on, up to ...

On the 12th day of Tories my PM gave to me
Twelve abolished freedoms,
Eleven phony briefings, Ten paid-for lordships,
Nine evaded questions, Eight Crony Contracts.
Seven broken pledges, Six blatant falsehoods,
Five blind eyes, Four new trade obstructions,
Three illegal favours, Two corrupt appointments,
And restrictions from which Tories all are free.

Come Fly MP ♪

Inspired by: *Come Fly With Me,* Frank Sinatra, and the video ends with a line from Delibes' Flower Duet
Augusta: It was revealed that Liz Truss took a private jet costing over £500,000 at tax payers' expense to do her trade deals in Australia. It was later revealed she had previously said, public officials should fly economy to save tax payers' money.
Side note: the Australia deal was particularly bad news for UK farmers. Brexit bites again.
28 January 2022

 Come fly MP,
Jets fly, let's fly away. (£500k)
Truss could use some cheese and booze,
From Dubai to far Sydney.
She cries with glee, we'll fly, make voters pay.
(Another Tory day)

Come fly with me, she gloats no airport queues,
(Private air cabin crew, nice)
In la la land, she's a Thatcher stan.
Such a cute trade route just for you,
(Farmers are screwed).
Multiply with me, emissions CO2.
(500 tonnes. Don't look up)

Rule Breaker ♪

Inspired by: *Heartbreaker,* Pat Benatar

Augusta: An ode to Owen Paterson recorded 3rd November 2021 after the Conservatives decided to try and dismantle all the rules to save MP Owen Paterson from having to face recriminations after he was found guilty of breaking lobbying rules. He could have just faced a 30 day penalty, but the uproar from the public on the vote to change the rules which passed with a majority (albeit with some rebellion) became the bigger story and within 24hrs he had resigned.

He's a rule breaker,
Sleaze maker,
Cash taker.
How does he get off scot free?

Lobby breaker,
Money maker,
Truth faker.
They all mess around with our dough.

Terms And Conditions For Prime Minister's Questions ≜

Mike: Mr Curtis Lee-Smugg explained the basis of Prime Minister's Questions.

Scan this QR code to hear his account of the Terms and Conditions,

Blackmail of His MPs ♪

Inspired by: *Female of the Species,* Space

Augusta: A whole flurry of bills, including the controversial Police Bill, were shot down by the House of Lords, whilst news broke of the Whips threatening MPs with lack of funding for their constituencies if they didn't support Boris Johnson with their votes, 21st January 2022.

A hundred thundering MPs await him,
Facing insurmountable Lords, lately.
And blackmail of his MPs
constituency for sale.*

No shock, shock horror at his dishonour,
He shouts himself hoarse,
Shows no signs of remorse.
And blackmail of his MPs,
When will they all go to jail? (Not soon enough)

He threatens their bank drafts,
Just one Whip, and they're zapped oh,
How does he face all of his MPs?
When a guy like him is full of lies and sleaze.

This oppression has this country on its knees,
When will we get rid of all the Tories please?
Pretty please.
(But not that Priti, no thank you!)

*Originally sang upscale.

The People's Protest ♪

Inspired by: *Simply the Best,* Tina Turner

Augusta: A parody requested by Take Back Democracy organiser Sharron-Lee Honey to help publicise their protest in London, with events also running online, recorded 15 February for their protest on 19 February 2022.

They break all their promises, and ruin our dreams.
(Levelling up, Brexit, see a theme?)
Speak the language of lies.
Truth? They don't know what it means.
(How are those questionnaires going?)
Mmm and it's all so wrong,
(Every day)
Take a stand and come along.

The People's Protest.
(This Saturday, midday)
Come and say you're not impressed. (Understatement)
Better get the Tories gone. (#UnitedAgainstJohnson)
This pain we won't forget.
If this breaks your heart.
(Let the bodies pile high)
Don't trust a word they say. (Ever)
Come play your part.
(Parliament Square or online)
#TakeBackDemocracy instead.

Bang a Gong, Get Johnson Gone ♪

Inspired by: *Bang a Gong (Get It On),*
Marc Bolan and T.Rex

 Augusta: Here is another song, 18th February, to plug Take Back Democracy's protest the next day. The coverage got a boost by a retweet by Hugh Grant with a fist-bump emoji.

They're all dirty damn cheats,
Need the sack, we fight back,
Did you see Hugh?
A fist-bump tweet, oh yeah!
(Now we make the news)

Life is grim and it's bleak,
And I'm losing some sleep.
How about you?
The dirty cheats all ruin this world.
(But come on Saturday)

Drum along, bang a gong,
Get Johnson gone.
(Drumming's at 12pm)
They're so wrong, bring it on,
Get the Tories gone.

Loser ♪

Inspired by: *Loser*, Beck

*Augusta: The "no sweat" Duke of York settled his
sexual assault case out of court reputedly paying
Virginia Giuffre around £10 million, plus another
£2 million to the claimant's charity.*

All done behind closed doors.
Is the loser sweaty?
Please, please don't sue me.
Spend a few million more.
An abuser, maybe?
But you can't say he's guilty.

Their Brexit – Going Well?
Sitting in What's Left of UK

Inspired by: *Sitting on the Dock of the Bay*

Sitting now that "Brexit's Done"
I'm sitting in diminished Kingdom,
Watching - I can't believe still
That's the Government with hands in the till.

I'm sitting in what's left of UK,
Watching our rights roll away.
Oh I'm just sitting in what's left of UK;
Don't waste time.

Had to get up and out and be seen,
Headed for the street, have my say.
'Cause we've had our rights taken away;
Looks like nothing's gonna go our way.

I'm sitting in what's left of UK
Watching our rights roll away.
Oh I'm just sitting in what's left of UK;
Don't waste time.

Looks like it's all gonna change,
And nothing still remains the same.

I can't do what Tories tell me to do,
So protest is the name of the game, yes.

Sitting here watching Happy Fish,
I went shopping and there I bought a
Turnip as that's all that there was,
Except ice made with British water.

I can't sit in what's left of UK,
Watching our rights roll away.
Oh I can't sit in what's left of UK,
Don't waste time.

Whistling

Lord Toritoi's assessments

Mike: Lord Toritori came into public view during 2021 with his assessments of Procurements, Brexit, Boris Johnson etc.
There were no scripts for the Lord Toritori videograms, but I have recorded here what the noble Lord said, and have made only occasional light-touch deletions to reduce repetition a little, but retain Lord Toritori's meaning.

Brexit is Going Fine

Oh hello.
Well, somebody suggested I should do
a little bit of an update about how
Brexit is going, because, there's been a
lot of kerfuffle about shellfish.
Fair enough, you can't export shellfish,
but frankly, do you want to export shellfish?
I don't.

So, there you are you see, for the ordinary man,
or servant on the Clapham Street, it's not really a
problem.
So the Brexit is all going pretty well apart from the
shellfish and parcels.
Apparently you can't get parcels to or from the
European Union.
But they're bringing somebody in,
they're bringing in Lord David Frost
and he's going to sort out any little contretemps.
I don't know how these arose really.
I hope whoever was in charge of the previous
negotiations, hope they've given him the boot.
Anyway, Lord David will sort it out,
and I say it's basically all right except for shellfish and
parcels and oh yes, Northern Ireland.
I'm afraid Boris dropped a bollock himself there
and didn't really know what he was doing,
but we'll get that sorted out.
So apart from shellfish and parcels and fish and
Northern Ireland and oh, other fish,
financial services.
(frustrated groan)
They can't sort out financial services properly.
So, it's all going to go to Amsterdam supposedly.
Huh! Not sure that's going to happen.
Anyway, up to Lord David.
So Brexit is going fine really, apart from shellfish,
parcels, other fish, Northern Ireland, financial
services.

And musicians, I understand, are having quite a
problem because they can't get their gear across
Europe, to different countries you see,
to do their pop concerts and so on.
Well, they could do a little bit more at home.
Same goes for shellfish I say.
Don't export the shellfish. We'll have more of it here.
So where was I?
I think apart from shellfish, parcels, Northern Ireland,
other fish, financial services, musicians.
Oh, and supply chains I understand are a little bit of a
difficulty.
I'm not quite sure what they are?
I use snow chains when we go skiing, right,
to drive in the car.
Anyway, whatever it is, supply chains have got a bit of
a problem.
Lord David will sort it out.
And really, I think if we could just align with the EU
on shellfish, parcels, Northern Ireland, other fish,
financial services, musicians, snow chains,
no, no, supply chains.
Oh and Grimsby!
Grimsby didn't want to be part of the new
arrangements with the European Union.
So, if we could just align with the European Union
on shellfish, Northern Ireland, parcels, other fish,
snow chains, musicians, financial services and
Grimsby,
then, ,,,
,,,,oh, perhaps it would just be better to rejoin?
What do you think?

Sovereign Tea ♪

Inspired by: *Yesterday*, The Beatles

Sovereign Tea -
There's no checks upon the Irish Sea,
Or there are the ones we said there'd be,
For Sovereign Tea,
Means we will see.

 Sovereign Tea -
So now we will decide we're free
To achieve what once came easily,
But now we try, negotiably.
Why we had to go,
I don't know, they'd not say yes.
Millions on a bus;
Let's discuss the NHS.

Sovereign Tea -
Nurses' pay's no easy raise today.
All the money's going Dido's way,
And so the staff, we cannot pay.
Why we had to go,
I don't know, they'd not say yes.
Millions on a bus;
Let's discuss the NHS.

Sovereign Tea -
Doctors' pay's no easy raise today;
All the money's going Dido's way,
And so the staff we cannot pay.
Ooh, ooh, ooh, ooh, Sovereignty.

Lord Toritori on Brexit and Football

Mike: These two sketches are remarkable in that the first one contained some complete nonsense about the impact of Brexit on football, which six days later was repeated by Boris Johnson at Prime Minister's Questions.
I had not realised that Mr Johnson was a Subscriber to the Lord Toritori "videograms".
22 April 2021.

Ah, yes. Lord Toritori here.
I thought I'd make a statement about football and Brexit and what a benefit that has been, that we've Brexited in the context of football.
Anyway, I'm making this videogram from the estate office.
We have this office in the old stable block where Nettlebed and the others work the computers for the Estate's doings.
Only thing is, it's bloody freezing here. I have to do something about that if I'm going to use this any more.
Anyway, football.
So, the English clubs have broken free from the straitjacket of the European Super League.
And they're free to play football in our own country according to our own laws, and a jolly good thing too.
And I don't think that would have happened if it wasn't for Brexit. I know there was no obvious connection but you would have found that would have been some directive issuing from the bureaucracy of Brussels that compelled them to play in the European League.

Luckily, we've got Brexit and so they're free to act on
their own cognisances.
And that's a jolly good thing, I say.
So, one up for Britain and they can be
in their own Leagues, promotion and relegation.
You see. According to merit, there's even, the, you
know, friends of mine who have, by the sweat of their
brow pulled themselves up with contracts, the NHS
and so on.
And that's merit. That's what we believe in, in Britain.
And I do want to stress, there have been some
references in the papers.
I do not have any shares in any companies supplying
contracts to the NHS.
Oh, what's that? Simpkins? Oh, hang on.
No, no, *(exits)* no, no, no.
Those are all in Lady Magnolia's name.
Yes. There you are. Yes. Sorry.
(Re-enters). Excuse me, just a bit of business I needed
to deal with.
Anyway, I have no personal interest in this at all,
but jolly good show for the British clubs and onward
and upward I say, and let's kick the Europeans into
touch.
Boris, Brexit, Britain, Brouhaha!
Jolly good.
I think that's all I've got to say about the football,
so you can stop watching.
Simpkins...come and turn this off, would you
and pour me a brandy?
Yes. Yes. Over here.
Thank you.

Brexit Enabled Our Clubs to Break Free from European Super League ⚽

So, good morning.

Toritori here, Lord Toritori.

Now then, there are those who have questioned the value
of these videograms, some people think I'm just a filly old sucker speaking to the camera, but I think we can now see the value.

A week ago, via these videograms,
I explained to you how Brexit has enabled the British clubs to break free from the European Super League.
I expect you saw it there first.

Yesterday, Prime Minister's Question Time,
Boris Johnson made exactly the same point.

So he is clearly a subscriber to this Channel and you could be, too, if you wanted to see more of these videograms.

You'd be well-informed, you see, ahead of time.
You'd see these things before even Boris Johnson uses them.

Oh, Simpkins. Do you think he's seen the one where I say Boris Johnson is a Total Arse? [1]
This could be slightly embarrassing.

Mind you, I think he understands that he is.
So that would probably be all right.

What do you think anyway?

Do give me your answers in the comments,
and I can respond to them, you see.

---

[1] See "More from Lord Toritori"

But anyway, Brexit has enabled the British clubs to break away from the European Super League.
You heard it from me.
Subsequently you've heard it from the Prime Minister.
You can see who's setting the trends.
And that's, that's everything really.
It's a simple point and I wish you a very good morning.
Simpkins, I think that'll certainly make them think.
Oh yes. Yes.
Yes, I think it's, it's just over here, isn't it?
I'm sure I could -
I, I'll, I'll be able to press this myself.
Yes.

More from Lord Toritori

Mike: Scan this QR code to hear more from Lord Toritori

A Simple Guide to the Benefits of Brexit Report

Mr Curtis Lee-Smugg

I'd like to give you a simple guide to the benefits of Brexit report.
Now this is a very impressive report. We told them it had to be at least 100 pages and they managed to come up with 101.

So firstly, we've done Brexit. So that's obviously a benefit in itself.

Page 8 - we've taken away freedom of movement.

But we have bought in the Turing scheme - page 13.

It's a bit like the old Erasmus scheme but not as good.

We're committed to achieving competitive advantage outside the EU Customs Union.

That's on page 58.

Thanks to Brexit, we've been able to check whether those trucks of Aid leaving the U.K. are valid to be sent. Before Brexit, they would have just gone straight through.

However, there are all sorts of things which we could do before Brexit which we can still do. So there you are. Stick that in your memes and tweet it, Remoaners.

Britain has quite a number of sectors of the economy and that made quite a lot of money before Brexit. Read about this from page 34 to page 100.

No idea what's going to happen afterwards.

But it might be more.

We are going to be able to stop all sorts of standardisation.

What could you do with that? The possibilities are endless.

I mean take the USB port for example we could make a special version of that called the UKSB port just for computers made in Britain. So, then people would have to buy one of our computers if they want the UKSB port.

Obviously, there are some crowning achievements already. And there are three which this report really highlights right at the start on pages 9 and 10.

I know it's obvious but of course without Brexit we wouldn't have been able to have blue passports (well, nearly blue) which are very different conditions to the old EU passport I can tell you, and imperial weights and measures and the crown stamp on pint glasses. So, I suppose that means you won't any more have to go down to the pub and ask for a litre of beer when that's more than you want to drink! Litres don't really work if you're buying a round, which is what we do in pubs in Britain.

And any financial regulations that the EU bring in - we won't have to follow them, page 14, giving much more freedom to our creative financial friends! Ideal.

You'll now be able to be uninsured when driving on private land - page 16. Restoring British freedoms.

We're expecting a lot more unicorns in post Brexit Britain - that's on page 40.

You just can't begin to count the Benefits of Brexit.

We have been reforming our public procurement rules - page 11 - so that the public sector does not have to go through some rigorous process to look for best value for money and can simply place the contracts with our chums who we know and trust.

We are entitled now to an independent sanctions policy - page 20, and that means that we can be particularly lenient on the Russian oligarchs whose funding is so important to the Conservative Party.

And as long as we resist any call to Rejoin the EU, we can continue to enjoy all these benefits.

More from Mr Curtis Lee-Smugg

Mike: Scan this QR code to hear more from Mr Curtis Lee-Smugg.

Lord Toritori, Finding Out What Brexit Was For

So, Lord Toritori here.
What was Brexit for, this is what we're now going to discover.

Scan the QR code to hear more

The Festival of Brexit
– now renamed *"Unboxed"*

Mike: The Festival of Brexit used an apparent budget of £120 million but made, as expected, very little impact. Attendance figures published in August were 238,000, so it would have been cheaper to give these people £500 each.

You can roll a Turd in Glitter,
But you cannot make it shine.
Well, they left us in the shitter.
Of repentance, not a sign,
As they head off with a titter,
Crony Contracts - they feel fine.
Please don't ask me if I'm bitter;
That defiant cry was mine.

The Brexit Game ⚖

Mike: Lord David Frost resigned, having failed to solve the problems that he had created, meanwhile blaming others. What a surprise.

 Reminder of the rules.

Step 1. The player to the Right of the Prime Minister starts. Let's assume this is you.

Step 2. Announce that it will be easy to get a great deal.

Step 3. Go to Brussels for your first negotiation meeting. No preparation is necessary, because if the EC gives you a great Deal as you expect, you would simply need to sign it, and they've probably got a pen there already.

Step 4. Announce that negotiations are becoming difficult.
Before we go to Step 5, there are some special rules which can be used at any time
- Kicking the can down the road is allowed at any time but it is no longer allowed to play a backstop - the rules were changed on that in 2019.
- There's a useful accessory - oh yes, the Brass Neck. If you have this then you can ignore any Deals already signed, any statements already made, and anything else you like.
Returning to the numbered steps.

Step 5. Declare a non-negotiable condition which you are sure the other side will not agree. This will save you from ever having to conclude an agreement.

Step 6. Announce that negotiations are close to a breakdown. Blame the EU.

Step 7. Resign, citing reasons that have nothing to do with the fact that you are not up to the job.

Step 8. The role then passes to the player to your Right. Repeat from Rule 2.

QUESTIONS

1. Who wins the game?

Nobody *wins*.

2 Then what is the point of the game?

Ah I think you misunderstand the game if you are
looking for a *point*, or a *purpose,* of The Game.
The Game is its own purpose.
It may of course create the illusion of career
enhancement for participants in their early gung-ho
phase.
But what it will do is, it will, if played in this way,
maintain the sense of conflict with the European
Union so that the Daily Express can fill its front-page
vilifying Brussels forever.
So, if you have this utilitarian view in which
everything has to have a purpose, then by all means
consider that to be the purpose of The Game.

- Mike Cashman and Augusta Lees -

Their Brexit and its Impact

Everybody Was Kung Fuel Fighting ♪

Inspired by: *Kung Fu Fighting,* Carl Douglas

Augusta: September 2021 saw panic buying at fuel stations across the country, with the south particularly hard hit. I was a bit slow at finding a parody inspiration for this but I eventually recorded a few days later 29th September. I didn't need to worry as the crisis continued for a couple of weeks. But don't mention Covid or Brexit, they certainly didn't have anything to do with the shortage of HGV drivers.

Everybody was Kung Fuel Fighting,
Pumps dry as fast as lightning,
In fact, it was a little bit frightening,
Brexit was such great timing.

There were grumpy irate men,
Driving all about the town.
They were cutting me up,
Running their fuel gauge down.

It's an ancient British art, (queuing)
Everybody played their part.*
When the panic buying hits,
It's enough to make you sick.

Everybody was Kung Fuel Fighting,

Petrol and diesel finding,
Maybe I'll take up cycling,
Boris where've you been hiding?

* Sang "held" instead, oops.
See my video for a high-tech sign at the end.
Blue Peter eat your heart out.

Close to Poo ♪

Inspired by: *Close to You*, The Carpenters
Augusta: This song came about after the recurring
news that water companies were routinely discharging
sewage into our seas all across the UK. The opening
line came from a tweet by Joanne G, recorded 26th
October 2021 after The House of Lords were trying to
force MPs to take action by amending the
Environment Bill that was being passed.
A strange state of affairs when the unelected House of
Lords were protecting the country and holding the
Government to account more effectively than our
elected MPs.

Why do turds suddenly appear,
When I look from the pier?
Who, like me, longs not to be,
Close to poo?

Why do friends come down with E.Coli?
Every time they swim by.
In the sea, there's lots of wee,
(Thanks MP)
From your loo.

Brexit Human Impact Scale ⚖

Good afternoon.

Here is the news.

An independent group, concerned at
the lack of measurement of the
human impact of Brexit, has devised
an independent scale for measurement of impact,
known as the Brexit Underlying Latent Level Scale
(Human Impact Test).

The scale has a series of numbered levels, each with a
brief description and an indication of symptoms. The
group has emphasised that the later levels will not
necessarily be experienced, but the scale has been
defined in order that we can understand what level we
are at any given time. The scale reads as follows.

0	Calm	In the EU	Normal conversations
1	Flickers Of Interest	Withdrawal Agreement signed	Newspaper headlines
2	Noticed	Trade and Cooperation Agreements signed	Daily Expresses waved in the streets.
3	Jubilant	British clubs leave European Super League project	Comic satirists and Boris Johnson attribute this to Brexit.

4	Diverted	Trade figures published	Population focused on when lockdown will end.
5	Infected	Johnson keeps open trade routes with India	Delta Variant spreads. Johnson says it's only small numbers.
6	Denial	Empty shelves in supermarkets	Supermarket food shortage disproved by Steve Blinkers from Much Blinding In The Marsh who publishes photos of full shelves.
7	Concerned	Nando's runs out of chicken and shuts restaurants	Fish, and chip consumption increases until there is no more cod.
8	Irate	McDonald's runs out of milkshakes	Package tours visiting Nando's and McDonald's in Northern Ireland increase in popularity.
9	Disbelief	No turkeys for Christmas	Objects start to be thrown at the television.

10	Furious	Food shortage bites	Food deliveries are mostly empty with occasional ridiculous substitutions.
11	Violent	Food deliveries grind to a halt	Because of lack of stock and assaults on delivery drivers from dissatisfied customers.
12	Gung Ho	Rationing introduced	Daily Express headlines about wartime spirit. Vera Lynn songs top of the charts.
13	Civil Unrest	Fights on the streets	Reality of rationing sinks in. Everybody very hungry. People assaulted for their food.
14	Bewildered	Dead cats abound	Cabinet Ministers indulge in orgy of dodgy photos affairs and dubious holidays. Nation stops to wonder what is going on.

15	Anarchy	Ministers don't return from holiday	Violence on streets while population tries to work out what's happening now.
16	Coup	Army takes over and brings in martial law	Emergency re-entry to Single Market and Customs Union under the EU conditions. Humanitarian Aid starts to flow to the UK from the EU. Free and fair elections announced within three months.

B.U.L.L.S.H.I.T. measurement 2021

So, I hope that scale is useful. As the group has said, it is an indication of the range of impacts, and there is no certainty at the moment that all levels will be experienced, but the scale is there to allow us to measure if those things occur.

I hope that's been helpful to you.

That's the end of the news for today.

Please subscribe to our news channel.

Thank you.

Bye Bye EU

Inspired by: *Bye Bye Love*, The Everly Brothers

Bye bye EU,
Bye bye trade success,
Hello Tory mess,
Elected on a lie.
Bye bye EU,
Bye bye frictionless,
Hello foolishness,
And more of us will die,
Bye bye good sense good bye.

There goes the EU, bye bye to you.
They're still united, we sure are blue.
We were full members, till Tories in;
Goodbye to good times. that might have been.

Bye bye EU,
Bye bye trade success,
Hello Tory mess,
Elected on a lie.
Bye bye EU,
Bye bye frictionless,
Hello foolishness,
And more of us will die,
Bye bye good sense good bye.

We're through with experts, we're through with facts;
These Tory cronies, get fake contracts.
If there's a reason why they feel free.
No competition, just VIP.

Bye bye EU,
Bye bye trade success,
Hello Tory mess,
Elected on a lie.
Bye bye EU,
Bye bye frictionless,
Hello foolishness,
And more of us will die.
Bye bye good sense good bye.
Bye bye EU goodbye.
Bye bye EU goodbye.
Bye bye EU goodbye.

The Army Greengrocer

Inspired by: *The British Grenadier*
Mike: It was proposed that the Army be called in to
help with getting supplies to supermarket shelves.

Some talk of David Sainsbury.
And some of Morrisons,
Of Asda and of Waitrose.
And doubtless other ones.
But of all these famous superstores,
There's none that e'er come closer,
Than a tow, heave ho, heave ho, heave ho,
From the Army Greengrocer.

None of these famous retailers
Maintained their own supplies,
Without the Army Grocer
With goods of ev'ry size.
But our brave lads do know it.

Will they give up now? No Sir!
Sing tow, heave ho, heave ho, heave ho,
For the Army Greengrocer.

Whenever they're commanded
To be the Tesco elves,
They'll haul the spuds and carrots,
And stock the Tesco shelves.
They'll march through every aisle;
Displays will be a show, sir.
Sing a tow, heave ho, heave ho, heave ho,
For the Army Greengrocer.

And when Brexit is over,
And trade has been unlocked.
The townsfolk cry "Hurrah, chaps.
The Army kept us stocked"
They're military heroes,
They worked hard. they're no posers,
Sing tow, heave ho, heave ho, heave ho.
For the Army Greengrocers.

So let us fill the glass now
And toast those who helped us,
Not those sat on their arse now,
Who made that useless bus.
But for the Army drivers.
Are we ungrateful? No Sir!
Sing tow, heave ho, heave ho, heave ho.
For the Army Greengrocer.

This Septic Isle ≢
Inspired by: *"This Sceptr'd Isle"*

Mike: I responded online to people who had not read the second verse and who asked me "Why do you hate the UK?"

This sorry state of things, this septic isle,
This den of crony works, this dreadful mess,
This other pigsty, this great fest'ring pile,
This coven of the knaves that won't confess.

 I speak not of the land and people fine,
But government that's in place by deceit.
That's had so many reasons to resign.
But sent integrity into retreat.

This open flouting of all moral rules,
For profit and backhanders they call fees;
This treatment of us as so many fools
They think won't see the wickedness and sleaze,
Or else will brush it off as "All act thus",
And tolerate wrongdoing with no qualms,
As p'litical manoeuvres on a bus,
Ignoring all the consequential harms;

This focus just on how much cash they hoard,
With ethical good standards in the bin;
That Ministerial Code that's just ignored,
With blind eye simply turned on any sin.
Determination that there'll be no lessons learned;

- Mike Cashman and Augusta Lees -

This attitude that rules are not for them,
That if you break the rules they're overturned,
That no wrongdoing will they e'er condemn;

This land with better past, this much loved land,
That had good reputation far and wide,
Is now leased out, by dirty oft bribed hand,
Like to a criminal that does not hide.

Britain, bound in with the triumphant sea,
Is falling fast, and left its soul behind
Contaminated now; as PPE
Has dodgy deals, and crony contract signed.

That Britain, with ambitions global claimed,
Hath made a shameful conquest of itself.
And never will the Government be blamed
For damage they have done to wealth and health;
Integrity's another empty shelf.

With thanks and apologies to William Shakespeare.

Stuck in the M20 Queue ♪

Inspired by: *Stuck in the Middle With You,*
Stealers Wheel
*Augusta: There were record queues on the A20 and
M20 near Dover due to the new checks required since
January. The Government desperately tried to spin
that Brexit wasn't the cause.*
23rd January 2022.

Well, he don't know why he sits here all night,
Got a feeling that something ain't right.
He's so scared if he forgets to declare,
Something that means he will U-turn right there.
Breakdowns to the left of him,
Smokers to the right,
In his cab, stuck in the M20 queue.

Yeah, it's thanks to us leaving the EU,
(Who knew?!)
And he's wondering what the hell he can do.
It's so hard to keep the smile on his face,
When the border stops have ruined this place.
Frowns to the left of him,
From blokes in the night,
In their cabs stuck, in the M20 queue.

When you vote leave and got Truss in,
Did you think this wouldn't wreck this man?
(Oh, but I didn't vote for that!)
And his friends all sick of hauling,
Beg and plead to just rejoin,
They say, "Please, Please".

The Shit Hits the Fans

Mike: An "original" poem.

So, it seems very strange he's PM of
these lands;
Well, his hair and his bluster
attracted some fans,
And Johnson said "Back us", though
he had no plans,
"I know that you're slackers, but all clap your hands,

As that's the reward for our brave NHS.
It's not Sunlit Uplands, but I won't confess.
If anything's wrong then you've done it yourselves;
There's plenty of fuel; there are no empty shelves.
If you think that this situation is rough
Then you should have prepared, there were warnings
enough,
And those warnings were accurate, it would appear,
Although at the time we called them 'Project Fear'

But now they're occurring, I think that we can
Just describe every warning as part of our plan.
There were those who raised some concerns of the
Borders.
When we said 'Ignore them', you should have
ignored us.
If you need a distraction from present day ills
Then I'll talk of high wages, I'll talk of high skills,
But don't mention burnt pigs or tomatoes that rot;
As Ms OakShott explains, be content with your lot.

Now I've given a speech,
Don't expect more from me.
You've got your blue passports,
You've got sovereignty"

Well, he thinks that approval for him's automatic.
But the fans are no longer completely ecstatic.
They see empty shelves and high energy bills,
And a benefit cut, while he talks of high skills.

But with Carrie he flies off, to work on their tans,
And meanwhile, at home, the shit hits the fans.

World King Boris and the Quest for the Sacred Benefits of Brexit ≢

Inspired by: *Monty Python and the Holy Grail – the French Castle*

World King Boris and the Ministers of the Tory Table travelled up hill and down dale going wherever they might to seek the true benefit of Brexit.

Steadfast, were they, in their creation of waivers, infringement of laws and kicking of tin cans down the highways and byways of their island home, concentrating only on their ancestral beliefs, handed down from father to son that one day, they would set eyes upon a benefit of Brexit, and then die. They were prepared to pursue that quest for 10 years or even 50 years as advised by the ancient wizard, Ree-Smugg, if they could but attain their heart's desire, one benefit of Brexit.

KING BORIS: Hello. Hello.

SOLDIER ON CASTLE BATTLEMENTS: Who is it?

KING: It is World King Boris. And these are my ministers of the Tory table. Whose castle is this?

SOLDIER: This is the castle of my master Monsieur Macron.

KING: Go and tell your master that we have been charged by the electorate with a sacred quest. If he will give us food and shelter for the night, he can join us in our quest for the benefits of Brexit.

SOLDIER: Well, I'll ask him, but I don't think he'll be very keen. He's already got similar benefits, you see, by being in the European Union.

KING: What! But the sacred benefits of Brexit are so wondrous that no man could even envisage them. Yea but that he seek after them for 50 years. As the wise wizard Ree-Smugg has told us.

SIR RAAB: But he says they've already got them.

KING: Are you sure he's already got the benefits?

SOLDIER: Oh yes, they're very nice.

SOLDIER *(to fellow-soldiers):* I told him we already got them.

KING: Well can we come up and have a look at the benefits?

SOLDIER: Of course not, you are English types.

KING: Well, what are you then?

SOLDIER: I'm French. Why do you think I have this outrageous accent, you silly world king?

SIR RAAB: What are you doing in England? I thought there was an English Channel.

SOLDIER: Mind your own business. We have settled status.

KING: If you will not show us the benefits, we shall take your benefits by force. Have at you with force majeure. Fetch the gunboats.

SOLDIER: You don't frighten us English, pig dogs. Go and boil your protocols, sons of a silly person. I blow my fish at you So-Called Boris king you and all your silly English ministers. *(blows raspberry)*

SIR GOVE: What a strange person.

KING: Now look here. My good foreign man.

SOLDIER: I don't want to talk to you no more, you empty-headed wallpaper money-spaffer. I fart in your general direction. Your career was a shambles and your pyjamas smelt of elderberries.

SIR RAAB: Is there somebody else up there we could talk to?

SOLDIER: No. Now go away. I shall taunt you a second time.

KING: Now this is your last chance. I've been more than reasonable.

SOLDIER: Fetchez la force majeure bovine!

OTHERS: Quoi?

SOLDIER Fetchez la force majeure bovine!
(Cow is catapulted towards Ministers)

KING: Hell's pyjamas, they're using force majeure
That's not fair.

Right. That does it. Prepare to charge.

KING & MINISTERS: *(singing as they attack the castle)*

Though our land this wrecks it,

We will worship Brexit,

We had to leave. So just believe.

We will never exit till benefits of Brexit,

A unicorn

Will still be born.

SIR GOVE: Aagh no, bird poo on my helmet.

SERF: Begging your pardon sir, you're the lucky one.
The bird shit is all around my head. It's all down my
hair. The shit has hit the man.

SIR GOVE: Impudent serf.

You are the fortunate fellow. That swallow has
relieved itself on my helmet and the excrement will
corrode the metal. The shit has hit the can.

KING: Run away, run away .. An effective retreat.
What shall we do now?

SIR FROST: Sir, I have a plan. Sir, we shall make a
second protocol.

You are now up to date with the continuing state of the
Brexit negotiations as Britain makes further
incompetent attempts towards a workable deal. This
time, it should be absolutely fine, we hope but could
anything yet go wrong? Will David Frost's second
protocol prove decisive?

Time will tell.

For the Leaders - So Where Do You Go To With Brexit?

Inspired by: *So Where Do You Go To, My Lovely?*
*Mike: I generally start writing by adapting the most
iconic part of the song, which here is the chorus.*

Well, you talked about 350 millions,
And said that could fund NHS,
That new trade could generate billions,
That we'd all flourish if we said "Yes", just said "Yes"
You said that we held all the cards then,
Did you even know what was the game?
You said they'd be begging for deals when
We left, with our trade just the same, yes you said.
So where do you go to with Brexit?
When benefits aren't what you said?
So, tell me why we had to exit?
Do you still have those thoughts in your head?
Are they there?

In your victory you looked so heady -
Said no more negotiation.
And you said that your Deal's Oven-Ready,
And you said you would Get Brexit Done,
Get it Done.
I've seen your extreme explanations;
I've seen that you know who to blame.
I've seen all your contrived orations,
That Remainers spoiled Brexit, a shame, yes it was.
So where do you go to with Brexit?
When benefits aren't what you said?

So, tell me why we had to exit?
Do you still have those thoughts in your head?
Are they there?

And benefits are what you're seeking,
As you didn't plan this in advance.
Do you keep a straight face while you're speaking,
Having left this entirely to chance, just to chance?
Well, I've read the report that's supposed to
Describe your great wins if you can,
Despite those of us who were opposed to
This, all see there's nowt in your plan, got no plan
So, where do you go to with Brexit?
When benefits aren't what you said?
So, tell me why we had to exit?
Do you still have those thoughts in your head?
Are they there?

As it's now two years on and you still don't
Know why we should suffer this mess,
Then I'm clear that forever you still won't
Acknowledge the shit and confess, and confess.
As the crops on the fields, they have rotted,
With workers in Britain so few,
So, after this time, have you spotted
That now we should Rejoin EU, yes, we should.

So, where do you go to with Brexit?
When benefits aren't what you said?
So tell me why we had to exit?
Do you still have those thoughts in your head?
Are they there?

Still There in Downing Street?

Nadine ♪

Inspired by: *Jolene*, Dolly Parton

Augusta: Nadine Dorries made a very bizarre Channel 4 News interview, a little wobbly, outside the chamber of the House of Commons, defending Johnson from the indefensible. The next day, pictures also appeared, from the debates, of her looking adoringly at him. For context, her appearance as a contestant on "I'm A Celebrity Get Me Out of Here" a few years ago means she enjoyed the delights of eating an ostrich anus.
3rd February 2022.

Nadine, Nadine, Nadine, Nadine,
We're begging of you leave, and take your man. (Ew)
Nadine, Nadine, Nadine, come clean,
Please don't defend him just because you can.
(Meanwhile at Channel 4 News…)

Your folly is beyond compare,
You're swaying lots with a manic stare,
A travesty from benches emerald green.
(Cue the memes)

Is this the end of his right wing?
Your neck's outstretched, are you in pain?
Is an ostrich anus worse than this, Nadine?
(Bottoms up!)

And you talk about him in your sleep,
And there's nothing you can do to keep,
From crying when rivals smear his name, Nadine.
(Currie/Major vibes)

And we can hardly understand,
Quite why you're his biggest fan,
But you've got no integrity, Nadine.

Nadine, Nadine, party smokescreen.
You take us all for fools, a Tory scam.
Nadine, Nadine, you're all obscene.
Please take them all away, a lifetime ban.

Or guillotine.
(Inadvertently)*

*A reminder that MPs cannot accuse others of lying in
the House of Commons, only of inadvertently
misleading. Ian Blackford refused to withdraw his
statement calling Boris Johnson a liar, so he walked
out before he was thrown out.*

SpAd Day ♪

Inspired by: *Bad Day,* Daniel Powter, and a song title suggestion by comedian Matt Green.

Augusta: Another flurry of special advisers (SpAds) resigned all in one day due to Johnson's continued past and present behaviour. More letters of no confidence had been filed from other MPs. But he, somehow, was still clinging on like a grotesque barnacle on the Titanic.
4th February 2022.

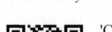

'Cause you had a SpAd day,
You're another one down,
I think I've lost count,
It's a quick turn around,

What do they all know?
You say you don't lie. (Ha!)
You work with a smirk, take us all for a ride.

Did you have a bad day?
The letters don't lie.
Will you ever stand down?
'Cause we're losing our minds.

But we'll wait for Sue Gray, (and The Met)
For your next bad day.

Keir Starmer ♪

Inspired by: *Firestarter,* The Prodigy

Augusta: Many times I've written ideas and not recorded, but this is the first time I recorded, but did not post anywhere at the time. But I thought the world was missing out on my heavy eyeliner and a kind of victory roll nod to Keith Flint's hair in the Firestarter video. Originally recorded 6th February 2022, after Labour announced their new slogan for Keir Starmer, 'No drama, just Starmer'.

He's the question asker, QC instigator.
PM's fear constricted, his dangers illustrated.
He is Keir Starmer, brutal truth imparter.
Boris hair of llama, can't wait for all his karma.
This is Keir Starmer, the no drama Starmer.

(Keith's rolling in his grave)

Toy Soldiers ♪

Inspired by: *Toy Soldiers*, Martika

Augusta: Still in office 7th February 2022, Boris Johnson declared a tank division will be needed to get him out of Downing Street. That didn't sound very democratic. Crowdfunding for tanks started soon after. Watch for a bonus ending.

Tank by tank,
When does it start?
Left, right, left,
They'll all fall down. (Eventually)
Like Toy Soldiers.

I Have No Confidence ♪

Inspired by: *I Have Confidence,*
Rodgers and Hammerstein, *The Sound of Music,* and
brainstormed with Adam Fowle

Augusta: Public booing was following Boris Johnson around and becoming more widespread, very notably during the various events for the Queen's Platinum Jubilee. This was recorded the day after the no confidence vote held on 6th June 2022. The Prime Minister won, although 148 Conservative rebels was quite a side-swipe to his leadership.

148 have no confidence in that swine,
Not sure if the others have a brain?
I have confidence in the leadership
campaign,

As all signs from his MPs
There is no competence to see.
(What a Jubilee)

Strength doesn't lie in numbers. (Or lie at all)
Strength doesn't lie in wealth.
(From Russian donors)
Strength lies in nice and peaceful slumbers,
When you wake up.
'Break up!', thinks Carrie.

He trusts no one but his ego,
Maybe Nadine or Peter Bone?
He has confidence, but confidence alone.
And as you can see...
The booing public disagree.

Tory Criminals ♪

Inspired by: *Smooth Criminal*, Michael Jackson

*Augusta: The death knell of independent journalism
was tolling on the 20th June 2022, when it was
revealed that No.10 had tried to intervene on a story
The Times were running that Boris Johnson attempted
to install Carrie, when she was his mistress, into a
£100k a year position of Chief of Staff. This was
recorded a day later.*

Carrie are you OK?
Times full of hearsay.
Another bad day Carrie.
Nearly bumper payday.

Salary 100k.
Someone said, 'No way Carrie!'

I don't think it's OK,
Papers shouldn't be swayed.
Ethics decayed badly.

We've been hit by.
We've been struck by,
Tory Criminals.

Sex Pests and Liars ♪

Inspired by: *Sex on Fire,* Kings of Leon

Staying up to see the results of the two by-elections was uplifting. Two separate sex scandals involving Conservative MPs led to these elections, one for watching porn in the House of Commons and the other for assaulting a minor. In the early hours of 24th June Liberal Democrats won the super safe seat of Honiton and Tiverton and it was a Labour retake of Wakefield. However, this was really a victory for tactical voting as people 'lent' their votes to the party most likely to block the Conservative candidate.

The voters are swaying,
I like how that sounds,
The news we are watching,
Yeah we're watching.
(Hello all nighters)

What a commotion,

Defeated today. (Hard luck Hurford*)
Got people talking, (doing the double)
Yeah they're walking.

Out they go.
Those sex pests and liars.
(Well done tactical voters…as for Johnson)
He's doomed,
With what's just transpired.

(Early retirement?
Rwanda's nice this time of year.
Good morning.
Very good morning)

*It was a particularly tough night for Helen Hurford
who also locked herself in the dance studio of the
leisure centre where the votes were being counted.*

Their Parties

It's My Party, and I'll Lie if I Want To ≡

Inspired by: *It's My Party, and I'll Cry If I Want To*

Mike: A title that Augusta and I (independently at that point) could not resist.
September 2022 has seen public discussion over the question of whether it matters if deceiving Parliament was intentional. For anyone who might question the use of the phrase "I'll Lie if I Want to" in the title of this song, I refer you to the Sue Gray report and to Boris Johnson's statements in Parliament; extracts of both of these appear on the cover of this book.

It's my party, and I'll lie if I want to,
Lie if I want to,
Lie if I want to,
We'll all lie too, if it happens anew.

Nobody knows where the report has gone,
Cressida left the same time.
Why was she holding up things?
Well, she's supposed to be mine.

It's my party, and I'll lie if I want to,
Lie if I want to,
Lie if I want to,
We'll all lie too, if it happens anew.

Break all the restrictions, those are just for the plebs,
But leave me alone for a while.
'Til Rishi's well out of sight,
I've got no reason to smile.

It's my party, and I'll lie if I want to,
Lie if I want to,
Lie if I want to.
We'll all lie too, if it happens anew.

Carrie and Rishi just walked through the door
(Walked through the door).
No-one knows that we're here.
Oh, what a birthday surprise.
"Stay Alert" Oh no fear!

It's my party, and I'll lie if I want to,
Lie if I want to,
Lie if I want to,
We'll all lie too, if it happens anew.

Oh, it's my party, and I'll lie if I want to,
Lie if I want to,
Lie if I want to,
We'll all lie too, if it happens anew.
It's my party, and I'll lie if I want to.

It's His Party, and He'll Lie if He Wants To ♪

Inspired by: *It's My Party, and I'll Cry if I Want To.*
Lesley Gore
Augusta: After many strenuous assertions that he knew nothing about parties, or that parties never occurred, it turns out that Boris Johnson and up to 100 others were emailed an invite to a bring-your-own-booze drinks event in May 2020 during the first lockdown. Recorded in the early hours of 11 January 2022 after the story broke on the 10th.

It's his party and he'll lie if he wants to.
BYOB do,
Did they bring their own corkscrew?
One rule for them and another for you.
(Chin chin)

Apologise ♪

Inspired by: *Apologize, Timberland*

Augusta: This was my reaction to Boris Johnson after Prime Minister's Questions where he gave a non-apology for all the rule-breaking that happened on his watch. Recorded 13th January 2022.

He's up against the ropes,
Rivals sitting all around,
(Apart from Rishi in Ilfracombe)
I'm hearing what he says,

But I just can't make a sound. (Apart from swearing)

You tell us wait for Sue Gray,
Then you smirk and double down,
But wait, you didn't say, you're sorry,
Don't think we'll turn around and say, 'Yeah, OK'.

'Cause it's too late to apologise, it's too late.
(Has he even walked the wall?)*
I'm so sick of all the lies, he obfuscates.
Does he ever stop and think about their lives?**
Didn't get to say their last goodbyes.

I'm holding on to hope,
That his ship soon runs aground.

* I mention the National Covid Memorial Wall a few times in the parodies in this book. This refers to the wall of hearts - each one represents a life lost during the pandemic on the Albert Embankment in London.

** I found this a hard song to sing emotionally, and these two lines in particular kept upsetting me as I sang, If you watch the video you will see that, I couldn't look at the camera at this point.

BYOB ♪

Inspired by: *YMCA*, Village People

Augusta: Partygate continued to rumble on, revelation after revelation, often broken by journalist Pippa Crerar. It turned out the parties weren't one-offs but weekly affairs.
15th January 2022.

'Young aide, no, we're not in lockdown'
He said, 'Young aide, bring your suitcase around'
He said, 'Young aide, no The Met will not frown,
And we'll have to squeeze in Carrie.'

'Young aide, there's a place you can go,'
He said, 'Young aide, Co-op's just down the road,
You can go there, bring all the wine you can find,
And we'll say that it was overtime.'

'Friday night is for BYOB,
We'll put it onto your PAYE.
You can do anything, if you're an old Eton boy,
Bring on a DJ to make some noise.'

'It's fun to party when you're UK PM.
There really are no rules for us, just for them.'

How many months to come clean?
They partied through this ordeal.

So who will be the next one to squeal?
(Pippa, Peppa*, pig)
*Who could forget Johnson's visit to Peppa Pig
World, and his addled speech a day later, losing his
place (and the plot) and including an enthusiastic
anecdote of his visit.*

Boris the Liar ♪

Inspired by: *Boris the Spider,* The Who
*Augusta: If only I had seen Operation Red Meat (in
Veganuary?!) that day, 17th January 2022, I might
have been able to slip that in amidst,
Operation Save Big Dog, barricading
drunken Boris Johnson in during
lockdown parties, defunding the BBC,
and his penchant for hiding in a fridge
when tackled by journalists.*

Look who's up against the wall,
Blond and hairy rather small,
See the axe above his head,
Hanging by a little thread.

Boris the Liar, (probably not original)
When will he retire?

Drunk, and flailing on the floor,
Go and barricade the door.
Where's he gone now, we can't see?
Quick defund the BBC.

Boris' insiders,

Stitched up, higher than zip wires.

Creepy crawly, sneaky Tory,
Seedy, greedy, sleazy Tory,
Seedy, greedy, sleazy Tory.

When will come his sticky end?
Don't think this will ever mend.
No more fridges to be found. (Shame)
Who is next to claim his crown. (Eurgh)

Boris 'Big Dog' liar, (please)
Quite the dumpster fire.

Questionnaire Tonight ♪

Inspired by: *In the Air Tonight,* Phil Collins

Augusta: Partygate continued with the news that in the nick of time Boris Johnson returns his questionnaire to the Metropolitan police on the 18th February 2022. Next time I'm caught breaking the law I hope I will be afforded the same treatment and given a questionnaire. Maybe after a similar short survey I will be entered into a prize draw to win a Get Out Of Jail Free card.

Boris handed in his questionnaire tonight,
Oh Lord. (Oh Lord)

He's been waiting for this moment,
dobs in his wife,
'Cause he's bored.
(Has Russia invaded yet?)
Sue Gray checks his answers,
He swears they're all right,
Her reward, a lord.
(Sorry Baroness) *

* No honours have been conferred. Yet.

Tory Cakes ♪

Inspired by: *Baby Cakes,* 3 of a Kind
*Well timed, because a song that sampled this more
niche 90s song came out shortly after.*

*Augusta: Back in January Conor Burns MP tried to
explain away Johnson's rule breaking birthday party
by saying the Prime Minister was ambushed by cake.
Sharing pictures of cake that had ambushed you was
part of the online Take Back Democracy protest 19th
February 2022.*
*Eagle eyed viewers will spot my very own tea cake
ambush whilst playing, I'm glad I didn't get fined.*

Tory cakes, they ambush Bojo.
(Shocking)
They lie, lie,
But say they don't know, know.
(How convenient)

And I just wanted you to know that I think they all
should go.

We take it step by step,
Together we are not alone.
(Teacake?)

Where Is Sue Gray? ♪

Inspired by: *Fade to Gray,* Visage
13th March 2022

*Augusta: "Missing" posters were going up online for
Sue Gray whose report on the lockdown parties at
Downing Street was still surprisingly absent. It had
been completed in January 2022, but delayed because
of The Met police inquiries into the rule-breaking
parties. It was eventually released 25th May.*

One woman in her lonely spare room,
The case sitting by her side.
Those lies going cold, she's silent.
It's clear there's so much to hide.
(No surprise)

 Ah we await Sue Gray.
(So much delay)
Ah where is Sue Gray?
Où est Sue Gray?
(GCSE French)

Who Let Rees-Mogg Out? ♪

Inspired by: *Who Let the Dogs Out,* Baha Men

Augusta: Surprise, surprise, yet more Partygate. Rees-Mogg, who had been noticeably quiet up until this point, gave an interview on 18th March claiming that the rule breaking parties, along with 'wokery', was nonsense, trivial, and disproportionate fluff of politics. A hoarder's stack of tummy button fluff has more political integrity. 'Let the bodies pile high'.

The parties were nice,
The parties were pumping,
They sipped their Bordeaux.
The Tory MPs were having a ball,
A side order of snow. (Sniff)

We all stuck together started zoom calling,
We baked sourdough.
Jacob responds, so pitiful.
("Wokery's got to go")

Who let Rees-Mogg out?
Who, who?
Fluff you.

Red Wine ♪

2nd April 2022
Inspired by: *Red, Red Wine*
the UB40 cover of the Neil Diamond song
Augusta: The first Downing Street officials began to receive lockdown party fines. Members of the public organising gatherings had previously been ordered to pay £10,000 for a first offence if more than 30 people were present, £800 for more than 15, and £200 for smaller gatherings, not to mention individual fines for each separate offence. Systemic rule breaking by those that set the rules came with a special discount code SOZNo10 meaning they only had to pay £50.
The biggest April Fool of the year.

They drank red wine,
(By the suitcase load)
Justice is dead, (fifty pounds)
We won't forget that, why?
(Really why?)
Are the sums so low? (I wonder)

Misread their fines. (Where are the other noughts?!)
The Met says screw you, (if you paid £800)
All they can do, they've done. (Obviously)
These memories won't go, Bojo,
These memories won't go.

(Miscellaneous expenses? £50)

Nobody Told Me ♪

Inspired by: *Somebody Told Me,* The Killers, and thanks to a mashup of ideas with the comedian Matt Green.

18th January 2022

Augusta: Johnson was finally filmed wearing a mask when visiting a hospital during a pandemic. However, was this largely an attempt at hiding from continued journalistic questions on Partygate?

When pressed again his response was 'Nobody told me it was a party'.

'N, n nobody told me, that it was a party,'
That looked like a party,
That he had in most days in lockdown of last year.
Emails confidential, but they've got potential,
Of crushing him into the ground.

Happy Birthday ♪

Inspired by: *Happy Birthday,* Patty and Mildred Hill

Augusta: Partygate scandals continued, this time with the news that Boris Johnson had a birthday party during lockdown.

Happy birthday to me,
I think you all will agree,
That a party was essential...if your
name is Alexander Boris de Pfeffel.
And your mental age is 3.

(God's sake)

Sue Gray, Sue Gray ⚓

23rd February 2022
Inspired by: *The First Nowell*

Mike: When we were proof-reading Augusta questioned whether "Simon this Case" should be lowercase for "Case", but in this case of "case" or "Case", what case do you think should be used?

At first the PM his fury did show
At the cheese and wine parties where he didn't go,
As he didn't go to any such thing,
So, he got Simon Case investigating.
Sue Gray, Sue Gray, Simon Case make way
For investigation to be done by Sue Gray.

For Simon this Case, impartial was not,
As he'd held a party that he had forgot.
The probe he'd begun, he had to leave it,
And Sue Gray took over since she takes no shit.
No shit, no shit, no shit, no shit;
Bring in Sue Gray and then she'll report it.

And by the light of Sue Gray's explore,
The parties did multiply much more and more.
A suitcase of booze, and a vandalised swing,
Just at the time that our queen was grieving.
Sue Gray, Sue Gray, Sue Gray, Sue Gray.
They said her name to make it go away.

Sue Gray inquired with no favour and fear
With the Whatsapps and emails and photos so clear,
So clear to Sue Gray, she could write her report,
That contained, in its pages, every fact that it ought.
Sue Gray, Sue Gray, Sue Gray, Sue Gray.
They said her name to make it go away.

Then entered in Dame Cressida Dick,
Retrospectively now thought
Some charges would stick,
Would stick, the police their task would not shirk,
Especially as Sue Gray had done all the work.
Sue Gray, Sue Gray, Sue Gray, Sue Gray.
They said her name to make it go away.

Then they did obey The Met Police call -
Redacted, removed names and incidents all,
Until the report bugger all did say,
And was not what had been written
Down by Sue Gray.
Sue Gray, Sue Gray, Sue Gray, Sue Gray.
They said her name to make it go away.

How Much Is That Doggie in the Window? ♪

Inspired by: *How Much Is That Doggie in the Window? Patti Page and Bob Merrill*

20th April 2022.
Augusta: A GIF by Jon de Plume of Michael Fabricant's luscious locks inspired me to retweet this with an accompanying title.

By popular demand (at least three requests) I then
parodied the whole song later that night.

How much is that doggie in the window?
The one with the waggly tail.
He sits next to Moggy in that window,
(Look at him lying there)
I do hope that doggie's for sale.
(Or at least a large donation)

I must take a trip to California,
(Rishi sends his love)
And leave my poor sweetheart alone.
(Don't tell Nadine)
If he has a dog, he won't be lonesome.
(Put it on expenses)
And the doggie will have a good home.
(And a second one too)

Please throw all these doggies out the window.
(Big Dog first)
I'm sick of these scandalous tales.
(And non-apologies)
These doggies could find another window,
High up on the 4th floor of jail.

[And on the 5th May, remember,
A Tory isn't for life, so make it an early Christmas.] *

* A reference to the upcoming local elections across
the UK, which saw hundreds of Conservative losses.

It Was a Fine Day ♪

Inspired by: *It's a Fine Day*, Jane and Opus III's cover, at the suggestion and brainstorming of Adam Fowle

Augusta: More Partygate, this was written after it was revealed that more than 100 fixed penalty notices had been issued for parties at Downing Street on 13th May 2022. Boris Johnson, still, somehow, remained Prime Minister, with Rees-Mogg's assertion that the whole news coverage was a non-story.

Just another fine night tonight,
Probably some more crimes tomorrow.
(100 and counting)
Drank wine, through the night,
Now they pay the fines, but show no
sorrow. (Or accountability)

Remember that fine day,
Saw relatives through windows,
We stayed in our houses,
Hid tears with a short smile.

It was a fine day,
With photos out of windows.
They drank with their spouses,
But just for a short while.

They drank on the grass,
While our relatives passed.
Just look at this guy.

An impossible task,
She still wears her mask,
Look her in the eye.

He still won't resign,
But his end is nearer, tomorrow.

ABBA Tory Party Megamix ♪

Inspired by, in this order: *Gimme, Gimme, Gimme;*
Money, Money, Money; Mamma Mia; Dancing Queen
and *The Winner Takes It All* *
2 February 2022

Augusta: And yet more Partygate. One party held by
Carrie Johnson was ABBA-themed the night Dominic
Cummings resigned, at the Prime Minister's flat. It
was also revealed that there were raucous parties

before the Duke of Edinburgh's
funeral.
This makes the solitary picture of the
Queen mourning her husband alone at
St George's Chapel so much more
poignant.

Gimme, gimme, gimme, a party at midnight.
Won't somebody help me send Dom Cummings away.

Money, money, money, rules are funny,
('Cause you break them)
In a rich man's world.

Wine or Tequila, let's do shots again,
My, my, booze we can't resist you.

We were all drunk in quarantine, party scene, only
seventeen, oh yeah!
(Parties? Seventeen parties? Sixteen parties?
Are you keeping up?)

'Cause those sinners take it all,
Us losers feeling small,
We showed integrity, through Covid misery,
(We made a difference)

So will the Tory party fall? (Good question)

**Augusta: Many thanks to Ste Greenall for my first
parody air play of this on "The Full English Breakfast
Show", Black Cat Radio.*

Sorry Seems to Be the Hardest Word

Inspired by: *Sorry Seems to be the Hardest Word*
14 July 2022

*Mike: Boris Johnson's resignation speech blamed the
"herd", called the decision "eccentric" and said
"Them's the breaks", without apparently recognising
his part in bringing about his own downfall.*
What we got to do to make you sorry?
What we got to do to make you care?
What do we do when you don't worry
That nothing you ever do is fair?

What we got to do to make you sorry?
What we got to do to be heard?
What should you say when it's all over man?
Sorry seems to be the hardest word.

It's sad, so sad. It's a sad, sad situation.
And it's getting more and more absurd.
It's sad, so sad. Why don't you think it over?
For Boris Johnson,
Now, sorry seems to be your hardest word.

What we got to do to make you sorry?
Don't you know how high are the stakes?
What should you say when it's all over man?
Is all you've got to say just "Them's the breaks"?

It's sad, so sad. It's a sad, sad situation,
And it's pretty poor to blame "the herd".
It's sad, so sad. Don't call it "eccentric".
Oh, it seems to me
That sorry seems to be your hardest word.

Yeah Sorry! What we got to do to make you sorry?
What we got to do to be heard?
What do we do when you don't worry?
What we got to do? What we got to do?
Sorry seems to be your hardest word.

Sue Gray, No Fear ♪

Inspired by: *Santa Lucia*
23 May 2022
Mike: Thanks to Leon Berger for
singing this one. I saw a tweet from
someone who responded to the defence
"It was just ten minutes" with "What
would we have given to have ten
minutes with relatives who were dying?"
And the idea that people could not attend funerals to
bid farewell to close friends but Farewell Parties
could be held in Downing Street was outrageous and
insulting.

Bring your own booze today, clear invitations,
Bugger the Covid rules, damn regulations,
All welcome to attend, each dumb and dumber,
His Private Secretary invited all-comers.
Be careful of the Press, they mustn't hear,
Sue Gray, no fear,
Sue Gray, no fear.

PM was ignorant, this happened here,
Though he attended, let's have a beer.
"We got away with it", or so it appears.
Nobody saw the booze, so calm your fears.
"Comms risk" indeed it was, more parties here.
Sue Gray, no fear,
Sue Gray, no fear.

Party with booze and cake, he's pictured in it,
Saddened that he was caught, just for ten minutes.

That's why initially, he opted for lying.
Oh, for ten minutes, to spend with the dying.
We didn't have that time, couldn't go near,
Sue Gray, look here,
Sue Gray, look here.

Farewell at funerals, tightly restricted,
Farewells for leaving staff, they're not conflicted.
Junior staff were fined, as they attended,
PM was there as well, mercy extended;
Let others take the rap, police questionnaire.
Sue Gray, is that fair?
Sue Gray, is that fair?

WTF is an abbreviation.
For Wine Time Fridays, fixed invitation,
Suitcase of booze arrives,
Fridge for the wine and beer,
Distancing What The F,
Sit on their laps here.
Custodian says it's wrong; arrogant, we're,
Sue Gray, no fear,
Sue Gray, no fear.

Denied in Parliament,
"Parties? - there were none"
Attendees stupefied, shocked at what he has done,
"Rules they were followed, fully all times."
Let us not mention 100+ crimes.
Junior staff punishments, thought it was clear,
Sue Gray, no fear,
Sue Gray, no fear.

When staff would come to work, bins overflowing;
By photocopier, wine stains are showing,
Somebody very pissed, threw up in the garden,
Broke Wilfrid's swing, but gave no beg your pardon;
But the Prime Minister saw nothing here,
Sue Gray, no fear,
Sue Gray, no fear.

And the Prime Minister
Reads through the Report now,
Unfortunately, does not, resign as he ought now.
"Take responsibility" - not very clear.
Means WTF, it would appear.
He lies incessantly and he's still here.
Sue Gray, no fear,
Sue Gray, no fear.

Now we're discovering, she wrote what she thought,
But they discouraged her from her full report.
Party at Number 10, she showed some caution at,
Persuaded that further probe was not proportionate.
And so, we can assume, the worst's not here.
Sue Gray, in fear.
Sue Gray, in fear.

And if you're concerned, no action was taken,
New Ministerial Code shows you are mistaken.
Breaches of honesty and rank obfuscation -
These sins all previously meant resignation,
But the Prime Minister removes that fear.
Sue Gray, shed tears.
Sue Gray, shed tears.

Send In More Clowns

Send in the Boris Clowns

Inspired by: *Send in the Clowns*
Mike: A rework of a song from two years ago – with the same first line.

Won't we be rich?
It's not unfair.
Harding and Penrose in charge.
They're a right pair.
There are the clowns.

Billions are spaffed,
VIP Lane.
Give all our cronies the work
Again and again.
Where are the clowns?
We are the clowns.

And when we'd talked,
And signed up the Deal,,
Finally fixing the terms that we promised were real
Knowing we're cheating the voters, the EU, Red Wall
But did we care?
We didn't at all.

Don't you love farce?
My fault, I fear;
This country wants what I want
Though 'Spoons has no beer,
And where are the goods?

They see empty shelves,
And nothing is here.

Isn't it real?
And for the Deal.
Blaming the EU, 'cos that's what I feel.
But where are the clowns?
There ought to be clowns;
Don't worry, they're here.

We Need Net Zero ♪

Inspired by: *Holding Out for a Hero,* Bonnie Tyler

Augusta: Recorded 6th March the day after Nigel Farage launched a campaign in his words 'to kill of (sic) Boris Johnson's ruinous green agenda' and demand a referendum on Net Zero. It seems particularly pertinent that in the summer of 2022 the previous records for heat were smashed in multiple places across the UK and a drought declared in many areas after a second heatwave hit.

We need Net Zero,
But Nigel Farage our hero (!) thinks a
vote is now right,
(Is he paid in rubles?)
He's so bloody wrong, and we've
gotta act fast,

The pompous prat just spouts so much sh…tripe.
Don't feed his ego.
(Probably shouldn't have done a song)

When the Going Gets Tough ♪

Inspired by: *When the Going Gets Tough* Billy Ocean and *Largo,* from Dvořák's *New World* Symphony

Augusta: 2022 was a bumper year for sex scandals involving MPs. Conservative David Warburton (of the bread dynasty) was suspended from office 3rd April as claims of sexual harassment and drug use were investigated. The parody came about following an entirely fictional tweet that went viral. The tweet claimed Mr Warburton tried to explain that a picture of him next to a line of unidentified white powder was in fact dandruff. He did, however, get admitted into a

psychiatric hospital following his suspension, prompting many working in mental health to lament the horrific waiting list and underfunding of services in the NHS.

I got something to tell you,
(It's not what you think)
I got something to say.
(It's a bit personal)
I need some cream or some lotion,
(Or maybe some shampoo?)
Won't let it stand in my way.

'Cause when the going gets tough,
Dandruff starts snowing.

Gonna buy me a one way ticket,
(To a psychiatric unit)

Nothing's gonna to stand in my way.
(Because I went private)
Stop these accusations coming.
(I'm having a midlife crisis) *
I need to get my mental health back.
(I'm the real victim)

Darling, just a little dead skin mountain.
Darling, I didn't do anything. (Sniff)
When the going gets tough, the bluffs keep going.

[But in all seriousness, I think we can agree, that Hovis is better than Warburtons.]

* Sarah Vine gave an interview saying she felt sorry for him and that perhaps he was going through a mid-life crisis.

Non-Dom ♪

Inspired by: *Chopin's Funeral March* and a meme created by Captain Howdy posted on Twitter.

Augusta: News broke that Rishi Sunak's wife, Askharta Murty, avoided paying large sums of tax in the UK on her multimillionaire pound fortune due to her non-domicile status, whilst her husband was Chancellor of the Exchequer. More of a visual video with accompanying photos of Dominic Cummings, Nadine Dorries, Dominic Raab and Aksharta Murty. This was recorded a few days after the news broke on 10th April 2022.

Dom, Dim, Dim Dom.
Non-Dom, Dim Dom,
Dim, Non-Dom.

Rwanda ♪
Inspired by: *Africa,* Toto

Augusta: Recorded 15th April 2022 after Priti Patel launched her bold new initiative to send refugees to Rwanda for processing, a country where our Government had previously accused their Government of human rights violations. For the bargain price of £120 million pounds as an initial upfront fee to their Government, Patel thought this was an excellent idea to roll out. However, it turned out that she was advised against this, particularly as it might break International Human Rights Law, so it was no surprise that legal proceedings were immediately brought against the Government. Breaking International law sounds eerily familiar…

Priti's gonna drag refugees away from view,
 It will only cost a few hundred mil,
It's the least that she can do.
She'll now detain down in Rwanda,
Gonna say, 'What crime?'
And break the law, but it's really not
that bad.

(For like nine minutes or in a limited and specific way, it's, what's the word? Fine.)

The Sword of Truth Meets a Brave Knight...and Cuts His Limbs Off ≢

Inspired by: *Monty Python and the Holy Grail, the Black Knight*

[King Arthur music]

[music stops]

BLACK KNIGHT: Get!

[music stops]

BLACK KNIGHT: Brexit!

GREEN KNIGHT: Ooh!

[King Arthur music]

[music stops]

[stab]

BLACK KNIGHT: Done!

GREEN KNIGHT: Oh!

Ooh! Uuh.

BLACK KNIGHT: Take!

[clang]

BLACK KNIGHT and GREEN KNIGHT:

Oh!, etc.

BLACK KNIGHT: Back

GREEN KNIGHT: Aaaaaah! Aaaaaaaaah!

[woosh]

BLACK KNIGHT: Control

[BLACK KNIGHT kills GREEN KNIGHT]

[thud] [scrape]

BLACK KNIGHT: Umm!

[clop clop clop]

ARTHUR: You have fought strenuously, Sir Knight.

[pause]

I carry the Sword of Truth.

[pause]

I seek the finest and the bravest leaders in the world to join me.
[pause]
You have proved yourself worthy. Will you join me?
[pause – no response]
You make me sad. So be it. Come, Keir.
BLACK KNIGHT: Get Brexit Done.
ARTHUR: What?
BLACK KNIGHT: Get Brexit Done.
ARTHUR: I have no quarrel with you, good Sir Knight, but I must make progress.
BLACK KNIGHT: Then you shall die.
ARTHUR: I command you, with the Sword of Truth, to make way!
BLACK KNIGHT: Take Back Control.
ARTHUR: So be it!
ARTHUR and BLACK KNIGHT: Aaah!, Hiyaah! etc.
There's for your Crony Contracts
[ARTHUR chops the BLACK KNIGHT's left arm off]
ARTHUR: Now stand aside, worthy adversary.
BLACK KNIGHT: 'Tis but a scratch.
ARTHUR: A scratch? You've been shown up for enriching your cronies
BLACK KNIGHT: No, I haven't.
ARTHUR: Well, what's that wound, then? A proven deceit.
BLACK KNIGHT: I've had worse.
ARTHUR: You liar!
BLACK KNIGHT: Come on, you pansy!
[clang]
Huyah!
[clang]

Hiyaah!

[clang]

Aaaaaaaah!

[ARTHUR chops the BLACK KNIGHT's right arm off]

ARTHUR: That shows you cannot change the rules to suit your corrupt MPs!

[kneeling]

We thank Thee Lord, that in Thy mer--

BLACK KNIGHT: Hah!

[kick]

Come on, then.

ARTHUR: What?

BLACK KNIGHT: Have at you!

[kick]

ARTHUR: Eh. You are indeed bold, Sir Knight, but you are busted.

BLACK KNIGHT: Oh, had enough, eh?

ARTHUR: Look, you stupid bastard. You've been totally exposed.

BLACK KNIGHT: No, I haven't.

ARTHUR: Look!

BLACK KNIGHT: Just a flesh wound. You wanted to stop Brexit.

[kick]

ARTHUR: Look, stop that.

BLACK KNIGHT: Chicken!

[kick]

Chickennnn!

ARTHUR: Look, I'll have your leg. *[kick]*

Right! *[whop]*

[ARTHUR chops the BLACK KNIGHT's right leg off]

You have been exposed for breaking your own lockdown rules.

BLACK KNIGHT: I'll survive that,
I'm going to do you for that!

ARTHUR: You'll what?

BLACK KNIGHT: Come here!

ARTHUR: What are you going to do, infect me with the same problem?

BLACK KNIGHT: I'm invincible!

ARTHUR: You're a looney.

BLACK KNIGHT: The Black Knight always triumphs! Have at you! Come on, then.

[whop]

[ARTHUR chops the BLACK KNIGHT's left leg off]

ARTHUR: You have been exposed for lying to Parliament.

BLACK KNIGHT: Oh? All right, let's draw a line under this.

ARTHUR: Come, Keir.

BLACK KNIGHT: Oh. Oh, I see. Running away, eh? Get behind me while I deliver for the people of this country.

BLACK KNIGHT: The British people want me to carry on, doing whatever we are doing.

PEOPLE: No, we don't.

PEOPLE: Boo.

Susanna Takes You Down

Inspired by: *Suzanne Takes You Down*, Leonard
Cohen

*Mike: A pensioner called Brenda
travels on the buses during the day to
keep warm, Susanna Reid interviewed
the Prime Minister.*

Susanna takes you down
To the place where you shiver,
As you hear familiar questions,
As you're sitting there beside her,
And you know you have no answer,
And you wish you would not be there,
And she asks you if you're honest,
If from truth you are a hider.
And although now you should tell her
There's no answers you can give her,
Then she gets you on to Brenda,
And you struggle for an answer,
Must she always be a traveller?
You won't want to travel with her,
You try not to seem unkind,
But you know no-one will trust you.
You've besmirched a noble office with your mind.

And the Truth is going to fail you,
You can't walk upon the water,
Though you've spent a long time lying,
Spinning yarns away in India,
And when you thought for certain
That the voters still would back you,

You said MPs can be liars then,
And pleaded not to sack you.
But you had long presided,
With contracts for Tory greedy,
Not competed, just awarded
To the cronies who couldn't help the needy.
You won't want to travel with us,
You don't want to seem unkind,
But we know no-one will trust you.
You've besmirched a noble office with your mind.

Now Sue Gray makes you face up,
To the issues you won't answer
When you gave your bare-faced lies
When you're standing in the Chamber,
Said you're angry to discover
There were parties, what a chancer,
As you went to many of them,
You now struggle for disclaimer,
And you battle on attempting
To fulfil your crazy mission,
To stay on and take over
The Electoral Commission.
While Sue Gray holds the report.

You won't want to travel with us,
You don't want to seem unkind.
But you know no-one will trust you;
You've besmirched a noble office with your mind.

Land Of Hopeless Tories

Inspired by: *Land of Hope and Glory*

Land of hopeless Tories;
Problems they can't see.
How shall we remove them?
How fed up we will be.

Dido waster Dido -
Billions she would get.
Johnson made her mighty;
Built up national debt.

Land of hopeless Tories;
Problems they can't see.
How shall we remove them?
How fed up we will be.

Lied on, still, and lied on,
With no bounds they set.
Privilege their right. They
Think they're right here yet,
Privilege their right. They
Think they're right here yet.

The Pincher ♪

Inspired by: *The Winner Takes it All*, ABBA

Augusta: As the year progressed it looked like a bonus EP Sex Pests and Liars, may have to turn into an album. Chris Pincher resigned amid accusations of groping in early July 2022. He lost the whip but not immediately, there were accusations of double standards including from the former MP Neil Parish who had watched porn in the House of Commons, twice. I recorded this on the 4th July and a quick look at the news in September shows that although he quit government, he is still an MP. The mind boggles, and stories are now emerging from a Freedom of Information request that he wasn't properly vetted after all, when placed in the sensitive position of Deputy Chief Whip, also known as the 'welfare whip'.

The Pincher gropes some more,
Throw the loser out that door,
We need some new MPs,
With some integrity.
(Or at least not guilty of multiple
sexual assaults)

Tomorrow ♪

Inspired by *Tomorrow,* from *Annie*, Strouse and Charnin

Augusta: 5th July 2022 was a momentous political day. As two of Johnson's most high-profile cabinet

members resigned it set off an avalanche.
When I was recording into the early hours of the
morning it had hit 10 resignations from the night
before, but in total 63 out of 179 officials over the next
few days. Technically Sajid Javid handed in his
resignation first but that didn't scan so well.

So, Sunak got out, Saj followed,
Bet your bottom dollar that tomorrow,
More'll be gone.
(10 and counting...)

Just thinking about tomorrow,
Clear away the knobheads who bring sorrow, *
'Til there's none.
(Snap election?)

Boris struck with a day, betrayed, and lonely.
(Apart from Nads)
Who just sticks out her chin, and grins, and...
(Oh God let's just not go there)

The Sun'll come out tomorrow,
Headlines say he'll hang on, 'til tomorrow,
But he can't stay...
(Forever)

Tomorrow, tomorrow, we love ya, tomorrow.
His end can't be far away.

* Augusta: apologies for language; the sound-alike
with cobwebs was just too exquisite.

Hit the Road ♪

Inspired by: *Don't You Come Back,* Ray Charles

Augusta: I had been singing about what I thought was Boris Johnson's imminent removal since January 2022 and the day finally arrived 7th July. I think this was the first time some of my Twitter followers had seen me smile. Many thanks to Christopher Spencer (Cold War Steve) for his inspired collages.

Hit the road and pack,
And don't you come back,
No more decor, get out that door.
He'll need a new flat,
'Cause donors won't pay no more.

(What you say?!)
He's a toad and rat.
Should have been sacked.
No more encore, for Putin's whore.
You'll need a new hat,
'Cause Carrie met Zak next door.

Even Larry the cat got bored.
Now we wait for the leadership…war.

(Eurgh).

Nobody Does It Like Johnson ♪
Inspired by: *Nobody Does It Better,* Carly Simon

Celebrations were short lived because Johnson didn't resign with immediate effect; he said he would carry on as a caretaker. It definitely didn't have anything to do with wanting to hold his belated wedding reception at Chequers. A quick reschedule and his wedding party was rearranged at a benefactor's premises.

However, Johnson still managed to miss a COBRA meeting, as the UK faced an unprecedented heatwave with predicted record breaking 40 degree heat, threats of wildfires and excess deaths. He was later located by the press, at Chequers.

So Boris drank at Chequers.
(But it's not THAT wedding party, he cancelled)
COBRA makes him sad and depressed.
(A heatwave is a minor stress)
More bodies line up, is this déjà vu?
Maybe, start the next inquest.
(Let the bodies pile high)

Boris Johnson Fantasy

Inspired by: *Bohemian Rhapsody*
Mike: My first Brexit parody had used "Bohemian Rhapsody" back in 2016 for "Brexitian Fantasy", but the evident Boris Johnson fantasy meant that I needed to devise a new parody based on the same song.

Is there a new life?
Is this just fantasy?
Electoral landside,
Has hidden reality.
Open your eyes,
Look out for my lies, and see.
I'm just a PM, I need your sympathy,
Because it's EC done, EC go,
Ratings high, ratings low,
Any way the herd goes doesn't really matter
To me, to me.

Carrie,
Just said I'd go,
Had a gun against my head,
Them's the breaks,
And now I'm dead.
Rishi, life had just begun,
But now you've gone and thrown it all away
Rishi, oooh,
Didn't mean to make you go,
If I'm not back again this time tomorrow,
Carrie on, Carrie on as if nothing really matters.

Too late, my time has come,

Sends shivers down my spine,
Now Brady's on the line
Goodbye, everybody, I've got to go,
Gotta leave you all behind and face the truth.
Rishi, oooh,
I don't want to go,
I sometimes wish I'd never resigned at all.
I see a little Lord Cruddas of a man,
On petition. On petition, can you make a plandango!
When the herd is moving,
Nothing is that proving, me.

Head of NATO, Head of NATO,
What's my fate, oh? Quote some Plato,
Head of NATO, Lebedev – magnifico.

He's just the PM,
No-one say "Brexit".
He's just the PM,
With a messy exit.
Spare us, oh please, from this monstrosity.
EC done, EC go, do not let me go,
Oh Brexit! No, we will all let you go,
(Let him go!) Oh Brexit! We will all let you go.
(Let him go!) Oh Brexit! We will all let you go.
(Let him go!) Will all let you go.
(Let him go!) (Never) Never let him go.
(Let him go!) (Never) Let him go. (Let him go) Ah,
No, no, no, no, no, no, no.
Oh mama mia, mama mia, mama mia, let him go.
Lord Cruddas has a deal put aside for me, for me,
For me.

So, you think you can sack me and just say goodbye?
So, you think you can sack me and not tell me why?
Oh, Party, can I just have one more Party,
Just before I get out, before I get right outta here?
Nothing really matters. Except Sovereignty,
Nothing really matters,
Nothing really matters to me.
Any way the wind blows...

Sunak or Truss

So, after the lies on the bus
May and Johnson were foisted on us,
And since nothing was planned
Then the lie of the land
Left a choice between Sunak and Truss.

U-Turns ♪

Inspired by: *You Spin Me Right Round (Like a Record),* Dead or Alive

Augusta: The prospective leadership contenders had been whittled down to the final two. What a choice. Liz Truss and Rishi Sunak. They had the honour of being the two most parodied figures in my back catalogue other than Johnson, but I don't think that was a particularly good indictment. Truss was leading in the polls but did have a little wobble when she performed a screeching U-turn regarding a multi-billion pound policy which she had launched only hours before. Her levelling down approach to paying civil servants less depending on where they lived didn't get the reception she expected. Truss then appeared to deny any suggestion that she had U-turned, claiming instead that her policy had been misinterpreted".

4th August 2022.

U-turns she's right round, pay cut plans down,
Broken record Lizzy, no brain is found.
Cue spin, Thatcherite clown, Rishi rebounds.
Strike the scoreboard.
(Save me)
Next round, who's crowned?

Recession ♪

Inspired by: *Tradition,* Bock & Harnick, from *Fiddler on the Roof,*

Augusta: Without a mention of the B word, forecasters were predicting the UK was heading into a recession and double figure inflation. With spiralling energy bills and the price cap that should be protecting consumers being lifted repeatedly, the outlook for the autumn and winter was looking increasingly desperate. There was no hint of irony as the two leadership candidates argued over their approach to fix the current crisis that had been overseen by them both as cabinet members under Johnson.
5th August 2022.

Recession. Depression.
(Tories ask…)
"Next question!"

 Inflation. Starvation.
(How to strangle…)
A nation.

    Work day and night to scramble for a
living,
Good luck if you've children, you'll need more than
prayers.
Price caps squeezed tight, no heating in the house,
Who cares if you lose your homes?!

Politicians. Tradition.
(They show no…)
Contrition.

Petition, or sedition.
(A winter of…)
Attrition.

If I were a rich man
Rishi is that rich man.

(Aren't they all?)

Rishi Hood ♪

Inspired by: *Adventures of Robin Hood Theme,* Edwin Astley

Augusta: I tinkered with a tweet of the same song by @IamHappyToast (with permission).
6th August 2022.

Rishi Sunak was hit by a disastrous PR scandal of his own making as he was filmed at a Conservative Hustings in Tunbridge Wells saying he had been responsible for undoing Labour policies that diverted funds to deprived neighbourhoods. Cue many comparisons with a reverse Robin Hood.

Robbing good, in your hood, piles it into Kent.
Rishi Hood, odds not good,
Winning Number 10.
Gives to the bad,
From poor neighbourhoods,
Robbing good, in your hood, Rishi would.
(Catchy slogan)

Get Back Bojo ♪

Inspired by: *Get Back,* The Beatles

*Augusta: Boris Johnson, after his "resignation" * speech, continued on as Prime Minister in a caretaking role. However, his summer holidays* *consisted of almost back-to-back visits to Slovenia and Greece, and removal men came to Downing Street whilst he was away to remove the family's belongings to Chequers where it was announced he would see out of the rest of his time. Chequers was given to the country as a retreat to be used by the incumbent PM at weekends. Not for whole weeks, during emergencies such as the escalating cost of living crisis. It seems Boris Johnson continued to be good at taking, but not so much at caring. A certain hashtag came to prominence on Twitter during this time, which lead to the recording of this August 17th 2022.*

 Bojo is a man who likes a Russian donor.
On his hols he had a blast.
(Twice! I wonder who paid?)
Bojo's leaving home,
He clung on like a sarcoma,
On to Chequer's greener grass.
(Ooh! Staycation now)

Fat cat, failed hack,
Get back to work you blundering blonde.
He lacks, true facts,
Backtracks, and misery is prolonged.

(Fecal sack Bojo)

* Did anyone hear the word resign?

Augusta: There was a resurgence in the popularity of my "Close to Poo" video after the news was once again flooded with water companies discharging their raw sewage in rivers and seas across the country, just in time for everyone's summer holiday. Twitter was full to the brim of song suggestions.

Waterfalls ♪

Inspired by: *TLC,* and thanks to a tweet by Dr Amir Khan
23rd August 2022

Don't go bathing in waterfalls,
And please avoid the rivers and the lakes,
They are full of poo.
I know the Tories gonna shift blame,
And do nothing at all.
Can we get rid of them fast?
(Please)

At the River ♪

Inspired by: *Groove Armada,* and thanks to a tweet by Jim Whitehouse.
24th August 2022

If you're fond of sand dunes and rancid air,
Quaint little sewage is here and there.

Stuck in This Midden of Poo ♪

Inspired by: *Stuck in the Middle With You,* Stealers Wheel, and thanks to an idea by Michael Rosen.

Well I don't know why I swam here tonight,
Gotta feeling that something ain't right.
I'm so scared of what got into my hair,
And I'm wondering how I'll wash my swimwear.

It's brown to the left of me,
More floaters to the right.
Here I am stuck in this midden of poo.
Yeah, I'm wondering, if I'm ill who I'll sue.

And the Government do nothing,
And the water firms just don't give a damn.
(Public ownership anyone?)
And the profits keep on rolling,
We gotta get it back we say,
Please. Please.

You're The One That I Want ♪

(Affordable heating)
Inspired by: *You're The One That I Want,* John Farrar, Grease

Augusta: As the summer drew to a close and the price cap reached new heights, with ghastly predictions of the next rise in another 6 months. The thought of winter gave me shivers in multiple ways. I had bad

chilblains last year and into spring 2022, so I am not
looking forward to winter 22/23.
I got chilblains.
They're multiplying.
On my fingers and my toes.
From conditions underlying.
(My blood is not supplying)

Tory Cargoes

Inspired by: *Cargoes,* John Masefield
Mike: This was also inspired by a reference to
Masefield's "Cargoes" poem in one of Michael
Rosen's pithy "Boris to Mogg" letters online,
following which I couldn't resist penning this version.

Millionaire of Winchester, this distant gopher,
Talking up as Non-Dom in sunny Tunbridge Wells
With a marker of tax hikes,
Cunning bungs and level-ups,
Taken from deprived spots and urban hells.

Flaky Yorkshire poser coming from the Dress-Box,
Dipping through the costumes by the photo ops,
With a bluster of tax cuts,
Level downs and pay snips,
Twaddle-speak and piffle-chat which never stops.

Dirty British chancer, what a palm-greased broke prat,
Bluffing through the crisis in the mad parched days,
With a record of whine lies,
Old fails, pig-thick,
Dead-wood, graft-ware, and cheap trick plays.

A Righter Shade Of Fail ≑

Inspired by: *A Whiter Shade of Pale,* Procol Harum

 Mike: And so the Tory Party members were left with a choice of Sunak or Truss.
Both candidates were enthusiastic in their criticism of the way the country had been governed ... by them.

They skipped the fact check section,
Turned some nonsense into quotes,
I was feeling somewhat nauseous,
But they both called out for votes.
The room was stultifying
As our hopes all ebbed away,
When we called out for another question
For the claptrap that they'd say.

And so it was that painfully,
As the jokers told their tale,
That our prospects for the future
Turned a righter shade of "Fail".

She said she was in Leeds then,
And the truth was plain to see
That they suffered deprivation
In the reign of Mrs T.
In the eighteen years of Tories,
Said how bad their life had been;
You wondered if she realised
She had just trashed her heroine.

And so it was that painfully,
As the jokers told their tale,
That our prospects for the future
Turned a righter shade of "Fail".

And Rishi said "No tax cuts;
For today, that's where I stand"
And he's manfully explaining
That in time low tax is planned.
And then he said "I'm British;
For today, that's certainly,"
And he smiled a wee bit skittish.
But can't force her to agree,

And so it was that painfully.
As the jokers told their tale .
That our prospects for the future
Turned a righter shade of "Fail".

If poverty is riches,
If lying's what we mean,
And likewise, if treaties do not count,
Then dirt in truth is clean.
My brain by then like cardboard,
And their words made no more sense,
As they both described their failures,
As if done by someone else.

And so it was that painfully,
As the jokers told their tale,
That our prospects for the future
Turned a righter shade of "Fail".

Is There Anybody There?

Inspired by: *The Listeners*, Walter de la Mere

"Is there anybody there?", said electorate,
Knocking on the Tory door,
As the people sadly contemplated
The cap that was a cap no more.
And the bank pushed up all the interest,
As accounts went into the red,
And the people asked the question
then a second time,
"Can you give any help?" they said.
But no response came from the Tories,
No help for the people yet,
Save money from deprived urban areas,
For Tunbridge Wells, don't forget.
But only a host of Tory members,
Loving PM well over the hill,
Who's far away enjoying his holidays,
(And I wonder who paid the bill?)
Sat clapping the wild rantings from the hustings.
That showed the dire state of the Hall,
Rallying as if they'd been shaken,
By a radical Leader's new call.
And we felt in our hearts their strangeness,
Their stillness answering our cry,
And the PM talked nonsense about kettles;
I don't know in heaven's name why.

And we tragically asked of them again even
Louder, as if they could hear,
"Tell them we're here, and no one answered;

What is it about us you fear?"
Never the least stir made the Tories,
Though every word we spoke
Fell echoing through the shadowiness of the Party,
From those they labelled as "woke".
Will they hear the call for the elections?
Will they notice us as they should?
Will they spot that the numbers in the ballots
See them voted out – for good?

Yes, I Remember Johnson

Inspired by: *Adlestrop*, by Edward Thomas

Yes I remember Johnson
The name, because of the doom -
One day, the referendum he plotted
Was stolen. It was late June.

Tories hissed. Somehow, they changed their boss.
No one planned, ideas all lame.
Nothing was sensible. What we had
Was Johnson - only the name.

And whispering, blustering grand farce,
Plans incomplete and cockups - why?
No wit, less will, and only kick
The can to the clouds in blue sky.

And for some years a black time rang
As Johnson brought round him, incredibly,
Ministers of no great talent,
Till this all collapsed - no legacy.

Our Economy and How They Wrecked It

Oh Lizzy, Lizzy ♪

Inspired by: *Baby One More Time*, Britney Spears

Augusta: In the final days of the leadership race Liz Truss pulled out at the very last moment of a TV interview on the BBC by Nick Robinson. It left a gaping hole in the schedule which was filled by The One Show presenters and Nick Robinson discussing this last minute change. Her press team explained that she no longer had the time to appear on 'Our Next Prime Minister'. It seemed that the favourite to win the race didn't overly like scrutiny so close to the finish line.

Oh Lizzy, Lizzy,
It looks like the public know,
 (Can't hide this one)
That something isn't right here.

Oh busy Lizzy,
She really is scared to go, (for an interview)
She hides right out of sight, yeah.

Show me a leader unprepared, she,
Tells us, maybe,
She won't want to go where there's no applause.

Her hopelessness is killing me,
(God why?!)

I must confess, did not believe, she would lead.

No interviews to show her great mind,
But show her swine.
(Pork markets!)
Won't talk Lizzy, not got time.

(PMQs will be fun).

Kwasi's in the Sunlit Highlands ≝

Inspired by: *Lucy in the Sky with Diamonds*
Mike: Speculation was rife as to what Kwasi
Kwarteng was high on as he rocked on his seat and
grinned broadly while attending the
Queen's funeral. Perhaps he was
amused by how he was going to crash
the UK economy later that week.

Trickle yourself fantasy economics,
With widespread tax cuts and no more NI rise.
Somebody calls you, you answer quite slowly;
It's Liz Truss with her happy wide eyes.
Bankers with bonuses shouldn't be capped,
Towering over them all;
Look for the girl with the glint in her eye,
And you're gone.
😵 Kwasi's in the Sunlit Highlands
😵 Kwasi's in the Sunlit Highlands
😵 Kwasi's in the Sunlit Highlands
😵 Ah
Dose yourself up when you go to the Abbey
Wobble about as you laugh yourself sick.

Even Suella's disgusted you're happy;
She's sat next to you, what a pick.
    (Pick! I said "Pick")
Newspaper writers forget that you're present;
Behaviour does not get a word.
Rock on your chair as you're fully protected.
Or did you just slip out a t…..?
    (A tweet? Was that a tweet?)
☹ Kwasi's in the Sunlit Highlands x 3
☹ Ah
Trickle yourself in a role you're unfit for,
And sack the man who would spot that.
But some minor royal is there to forgive you;
Oh no, it's Liz Truss in a hat.
☹ Kwasi's in the Sunlit Highlands x 3
☹ Ah
☹ Kwasi's in the Sunlit Highlands x 3
☹ Ah
☹ Kwasi's in the Sunlit Highlands x 3
☹ Ah

Kwasi Contrarian ♪

Inspired by: *Karma Chameleon*, Culture Club

Augusta: Kwasi Kwarteng the new Chancellor of the Exchequer released a disastrous mini budget which rocked the markets. It led to an emergency £65 billion bond-buying programme to try and bring stability after nearly tanking the economy including putting entire pension funds at risk. Labour began to stride ahead in polls and when Kwarteng doubled down on his, plan for growth, the pound hit an historic low of £1.03 against the dollar. Kwarteng later admitted there had been some turbulence. It was safe to say that £45 billion of tax cuts did not go down as planned. Those shorting the pound however, might disagree. Thank you to David J White for the song suggestion.

Kwasi, Kwasi, Kwasi, Kwasi, Kwasi
contrarian, (sorry parliamentarian)
He comes and goes, (U-turn)
As MPs oppose. (Already?)

He thought it would be easy to get away with all his schemes.
45p (P45?)
See you 'n T…V (turbulence)

(Fasten your seatbelts. And wear a damn mask.*)

*One of my reminders to anyone listening that the pandemic isn't over with the fourth wave of the year gathering pace.

I do not like Kwasi Kwarteng

Mike: A personal view

I do not like Kwasi Kwarteng.
I thing he gets things very wrong.
I do not think exams he'd pass.
He misses out his OBRs.
I do not like this Abbey Clown.
I do not like his trickle down.

I do not like the things he'll say.
I do not like his give-away.
I do not like what he's reduced.
I do not like his bankers' boost.
I do not like Kwasi Kwarteng.
I hope he's not here very long.

The Lady is Ga Ga ♪

Inspired by: *Radio Ga Ga*, Queen

Augusta: Perhaps showing exactly why she bunked off her interview with Nick Robinson just before the leadership race finished, Liz Truss had a disastrous hour on various BBC local radio slots lasting around five minutes each. She was left fumbling for words and often descended into excruciatingly long pauses. Her worst bits were collected in videos across social media and I recorded this a day later 30th September 2022.

She had air-time,
Lost her grip on power. (Already)
Those journos had their finest hour. (In five minutes)
Local Radio.
(Worth the license fee alone)

 All is clear, this lady is gaga.
Totally cuckoo,
Persona non grata.
So, which someone will sack you?
(Place your bets)

I Might as Well Scrap Insane September ≑

Inspired by: *It Might as Well Rain Until September*
Mike: Liz Truss came to regret much of what she had done in September. But perhaps becoming Prime Minister was her biggest mistake.

What should I write?
What can I say?
How can I tell you how much I've pissed you?
Now whether they have been as nice as they can be,
Although it doesn't really matter much to me .
For all I've done yet in my first month as PM.
I might as well scrap insane September.

Went to the Abbey though they said that woman's who?
And Kwasi fell about and laughed the whole way through.
As far as I'm concerned, he'll do what he will do;
So I might as well scrap insane September.
My friends look forward to their bonuses so high
But top rate tax cut, we couldn't get it by
Now watch the crumbs that slowly trickle from the sky
September isn't any friend of mine

It doesn't matter if you're rich as muck right now;
I'd like to give you more, but only question's "How?".
I'm only living for the way I'm here to stay.
So I might as well scrap insane September, September, September
Oh I might as well scrap insane September.

Kwimericks

I always thought he was aloof
And indeed disconnected from truth
But could he do more
When he speaks from the floor
Than send borrowing costs through the roof?

Oh Kwasi, you've got to fly back.
You'll think that your presence I lack;
But although my new oath
Is for growth, growth and growth,
I'm eager to give you the sack.

Kwasi's Sacked ♪

Inspired by: *Back for Good*, Take That

Augusta: As The Good Law Project so perfectly put it 'There's a pint of milk in the Good Law Project office fridge that's lasted long than Kwasi Kwarteng's chancellorship.' Recorded on 14th October on the day Kwarteng was shown the door, he accepted Liz Truss' request for him to stand aside and was replaced with Jeremy Hunt.

Kwasi's sacked,
His budget's crap.
Liz Trussed him up for good,

He got it so wrong, so I'll sing his
swan song on his exit.

With hindsight he understood.
He can't come back.
They all backtrack.
Now Hunt is back for good.

(Well. Maybe he'll last 'til Christmas. But will she?)

Tofu or Not Tofu ≑

Inspired by: *Hamlet*, William Shakespeare

Mike: the "tofu-eating wokerati" earned Suella Braverman's scorn. She resigned – not because she broke security rules, but she was caught doing so, She then took the opportunity in her resignation letter to lecture Liz Truss on the necessity for resigning if one had made a mistake. The rest is history
...

Tofu, or not tofu, that is the question:
Whether 'tis nobler in this time to suffer
The taunts and charges of the wokerati,
Or to send news via gmail address,
And by forwarding leak it; to ask, to plead
Some more; and by that means, to try to get
Some advice, as a thousand sim'lar times
Sir John was sent to; 'tis a consummation
Against the country's wish. To spill, to leak,
To leak, mischanced to be, aye there's the rub,
For in that email sent, in time of dreams
(At least, that's when 'twas said, not after dawn),
Is why she shuffled off her senior post
With haughty letter, admonishing Truss,

Who was not yet offending in this case,
Though failing, flailing, crashing all elsewhere,
And she would bear the Whips and Scorns of time,
The fighters' taunt, their curiosity,
The pangs of despised men, as papers say,
The insolence of Office, as she spurns
Correcting markets with th'unworthy drops,
Until that boss was pedestall'd again,
Spake reasons why, but knew the reasons not,
Standing by her downward wooden spiral,
The jenga of her brief reign soon to fall,

Then came hotfoot from holiday once more
The one ejected in the mid-term time,
Rejected once again as is his wont
For lying about lying of his lies,
And thought he to root out a hundred friends
To back him for the post they sacked him from;
No conscience to make coward of this rogue
Till impact on his earnings made him frit.

Yet Sunak, still afear'd of ERG
Made overtures of deal to Leaky Sue,
And offered her the same post she had lost,
Despite the mordaunt frowns as Penny drops.
So enterprise of U.K. leader choice
Rewards the rogue, restored now to her post,
Unworthy bargain seeing her restored
With sins no more remembered.

*More about "Leaky Sue in "More from Augusta" at
the end of the songs,*

More Liz Atrussities and Other Chaos

Signed, Sealed, Deliver ♪

Inspired by: *Signed, Sealed, Delivered I'm Yours*, Stevie Wonder

Augusta: A short song to mark Liz Truss' appointment as Prime Minister on the 6th September 2022 the day she met the Queen at Balmoral, and was officially asked to form a government. Truss beat Rishi Sunak 57.4-42.6% by Conservative party members, and her penchant for the word 'deliver' during the leadership race was continued in her first speech. Some likened her blinking during tough questions in the preceding weeks to needing a quick reboot. A rabbit in the headlights also springs to mind.

Oh Lizzy, she's PM.
Signed, sealed, deliver…
Deliver, deliver.
Deliver.
Deliver.

(Oh Lord. We're screwed.)

So Long, Farewell ♪

Inspired by: *So Long, Farewell*, Rodgers and Hammerstein from *The Sound of Music*

 Augusta: The day after Liz Truss was formally appointed, she got to work ridding the cabinet of all the Rishi Sunak supporters. A few of the big names that were headed for the backbenchers were *Dominic Raab, Priti Patel and Grant Shapps. Watch the video for a few more familiar faces who walked the plank. Recorded in the early hours of 8th September 2022.*

There's a sad overhanging on the walk to Whitehall,
She expels all the people, who,
Wound up little Lizzy the absurd little turd,
So she'd popping up to say, 'Yoohoo,
You're through, $&!@ you'

Regretfully she tells us,
No job under Liz Truss,
So say goodbye and screw you.
'So long farewell, auf Wiedersehen, adieu,
Adieu, adieu, to yieu and yieu and yieu.'

'(And you)'

This Pen Is Lame ♪

Inspired by: *Penny Lane*, The Beatles

Augusta: Two days after Liz Truss made the journey to Balmoral to meet the Queen, the news broke that the Queen had passed away 8th September 2022 aged 96. King Charles in his first week as the new monarch, unfortunately had two pen-related mishaps: one pen holder that was in the way and a leaky one that inspired this micro parody.

This pen is lame, just let me grieve
with no more autographs.

They Just Want to Hold Hands ♪

Inspired by: *I Want to Hold Your Hand*, The Beatles

Augusta: After the Duke and Duchess of Sussex had the audacity to hold hands in Westminster Hall during the procession of the Queen's coffin, they were met with press and social media ridicule. The hypocrisy when other royals also held hands including Mike and Zara Tindall was outrageous enough for me to record a song on the 16th September 2022. Thank you to Sam Williams for the song suggestion.

Oh I, am missing something,
'Cause I don't understand.

All I, see is comfort in,
(Grief)
They just wanna hold hands.

They just want to hold hands.
Look who also held hands.
[Reference to a picture in the accompanying video of a very senior royal breaking supposed protocol.]

The Queue ♪

Inspired by: *I Just Called to Say I Love You*, Stevie Wonder, followed by *Never Gonna Give You Up*, Rick Astley

Augusta: The death of the Queen led to quite possibly one of the most British sights we have seen this century; an orderly queue to see the Queen lying in state. It even warranted its own personalised weather forecast on the BBC. At its peak it stretched over 10 miles with a wait and walk time of 25 hours, and an estimated 250,000 people passed by the coffin during those six days.

 I just walked this way,
Now I'm in The Queue.

[15 hours later]

Never gonna give Queue up,
Just wish I could sit down.

Another Holiday

Inspired by: *Summer Holiday*, Cliff Richard
Mike: Boris Johnson continued in the office of an MP after his resignation as PM. It seemed that he continued to conduct his duties mainly from the beach.

Johnson having yet another holiday
No more working as PM, that's through
Who is paying for this other holiday?
No more worries 'bout me or you
For a month or two.

Ra Ra, I Love Putin ♪

Inspired by: *Rasputin*, Boney M

Augusta: Boris Johnson on the back benches let out an epic Freudian slip thanking the Russian leader Vladimir Putin for his 'inspirational leadership' in a House of Commons debate before quickly correcting to Ukraine's leader Volodymyr Zelensky instead. This was recorded 23rd September when Russia was escalating its assault against the capital Kyiv and calling for partial mobilisation.

Ra, ra, I love Putin,
A nicer guy I've never seen.

(Oops! Did I say that out loud?
Блядь*)

*apologies to Russian speakers

Liz Truss Has Got a Little List

Inspired by: *I've Got a Little List*, Gilbert & Sullivan, from *The Mikado*,

Mike: An adaptation of an adaptation. I had previously written this song for Boris Johnson, and I admit I kept some of his dislikes, but there were many new ones for Liz Truss.

1
As some days it may happen
That a victim must be found,
I've got a little list,
I've got a little list,

Of anti-growth-ish bodies where
I do not like their sound.
They never would be missed.
They never would be missed.

Deniers of the Brexit
Which we know gave us control,
And Irish-sea-bound customs-checkers,
Johnson's clear own goal,
The people who remind me
They said the Budget's wrong,
And poets like Mike Cashman
Who put all my words in song.

There's fiscal orthodoxifists
Whose fears I have dismissed.
They never would be missed.
They never would be missed.

Chorus: She's got 'em on the list.
She's got 'em on the list.
And they'd none of them be missed.
They'd none of them be missed.

2
The fiscally conservative,
With balanced budget plea
The arithmeticist
I've got them on the list.

The Office of the Budget - what? -
Responsibility
They never would be missed.
They never would be missed.

Intransigent North Londoners
Who taxi into town
Deliberately to criticise
And do the budget down.
The Treasury who just say "But"
And give reactions mixed,
And critics that can't take a cut
And want the top rate fixed.

Protesters at our conference
Who think our arms they'll twist;
That never would be missed.
That never would be missed.

Chorus: She's got 'em on the list.

She's got 'em on the list.
And they'd none of them be missed.
They'd none of them be missed.

3
The independent commenter
Says Kwasi's a con-man,
The nosy journalist!
I've got him on the list.

And Laura Kuenssberg asking me
Who voted for my plan.
She never would be missed.
She never would be missed,

Environmental activists
Disrupting building more
That chain up to the railings
The ceiling and the floor.
The militant bad unionists
I really do not like,
Who just because their pay is small
Think they can go on strike

And anyone who thinks they can
The Tory rule resist;
I don't think they'd be missed.
I'm sure they'd not be missed.

Chorus: She's got 'em on the list.
She's got 'em on the list.
And they'd none of them be missed.

They'd none of them be missed.

4
There's Conor Burns I have just sacked
Was naughty in the lift.
He was perhaps too pissed!
I put him on the list.

The Anti-Groping Coalition
Make me very miffed.
They never would be missed.
They never would be missed.

The enemies of enterprise,
The people in the hall.
And anyone with some surprise
Which makes me feel small.
The lady asking questions,
That make me stop and stare.
That make it very difficult
Which really isn't fair.

Climate-change reductions from
Th' environmentalist.
They never would be missed.
They never would be missed.

Chorus: She's got 'em on the list.
She's got 'em on the list.
And they'd none of them be missed.
They'd none of them be missed.

5
The heads of other countries,
Who are in a club we're not
Internationalist!
I've got them on the list.

Independent think-tanks,
And the Robert Peston lot.
They never would be missed.
They never would be missed.

The Scottish, Irish, Welsh and more,
Who will not take my rule.
And anyone on Sky TV
That says I am a fool.
And nationalist candidates
Not fit to hold our coats,
Who stand in our elections
Just to steal the Tory votes.

And then the Labour Party,
Who are simply Bolshevist.
I don't think they'd be missed.
I'm sure they not be missed.

Chorus: You may put 'em on the list.
You may put 'em on the list.
And they'd none of them be missed.
They'd none of them be missed.

She Has a Dream ♪

Inspired by: *I Have a Dream*, ABBA

Augusta: Suella Braverman the new Home Secretary starts to make Priti Patel look moderate as she confesses her obsession and dream is to send asylum seekers to Rwanda at a Conservative party conference.

She has a dream, of planes flying.
(To Rwanda! What a kind soul.)
No help, nor hope, from this Right Wing.
(Apart from incompetence)

It really makes you wonder,
If she'll write for the Daily Mail.
(When she's sacked)
'Cause looking to the future, soon they all must fail*.
(But what will they wreck in the meantime?)

She's their Leaver's angel,
Nothing good from this, her racist spree.
If she saw a Christmas angel.
She'd say, 'We've got no time for refugees.
Don't cross our streams.
We'll deport your dreams.'

* I don't think either Mike or I realised quite how quickly this would come true.

Dream, Dream of Rwanda

Inspired by *Dream, Dream, Dream*
Dream, dream, dream, dream,
Dream, dream, dream, dream,
When I want them in Rwanda
When I want to the Far Right pander
Whenever I want it, all I have to do is
Dream, dream, dream, dream
When I feel blue and must resign
And I need you to hear my line
Whenever I want to
All I have to do is dream.
I can be PM, get in power again,
Some time soon, one fine day
Only trouble is, gee whizz
I'm dreamin' my life away
I need you so, dear ERG
I love you so you'll vote for me
Whenever I want this, all I have to do is
Dream, dream, dream, dream, dream.
I can be PM, get in power again,
Some time soon, one fine day
Only trouble is, gee whizz
I'm dreamin' my life away
I need you so, dear ERG
I love you so you'll vote for me
Whenever I want this, all I have to do is
Dream, dream, dream, dream, dream.
Dream, dream, dream, dream.
Dream, dream, dream, dream.
Dream, dream, dream, dream.
Dream, dream, dream, dream.

Tory Fiasco ♪

Inspired by: *Disco Inferno*, The Trammps

Augusta: The news and scandals were moving at such breakneck speed that I was truly embracing the micro parody. This was recorded on 8th October after the news that trade minister Conor Burns was sacked and suspended as an MP after an incident of 'inappropriate behaviour' at the Conservative party conference. It won't be too long before I really do have a whole album just for Sex Pests and Liars.

Burns, Conor burns,
Another Tory fiasco,
Squirms and U-turns.
Watch them burn themselves down.

[Candle not essential]

Lettuce Leaf Will Entertain You ♪

Inspired by: *Let Me Entertain You*, Robbie Williams

Augusta: If you thought that the peak Britishness of 'The Queue' couldn't be topped, then drum roll for The Daily Star's livestream lettuce. Liz Truss's grip on power was being shredded daily if not hourly and the paper asked if an iceberg lettuce might outlast Liz's time as Prime Minister. Cue many salad puns, and I decided to commemorate this key political moment with a song dedicated to the lettuce on 17th October 2022.

 Lettuce leaf we can't explain you.
(To the rest of the world)
Lettuce leaf you're in full frame view.
(Could be our best British export since 'The Queue')

Her strife is short, we'll say goodbye.
Rishi needs an alibi,
Heaven knows they all just lie.
Mon Cher.
(Dear, oh dear)*

She don't know her right from wrong,
How long will this string along?
The kettle's on so don't be too long.
Don't despair.
(Too much)

So come on Lettuce leaf will entertain you.
(One wilt at a time)
Lettuce Liz are you romaine too?
(Oh! Don't mention the B word.
Butterhead.)

*A reference to King Charles's televised remark as he met Liz Truss 'Back again? Dear oh dear.'

Suella de Vil ♪

Inspired by: *Cruella de Vil*, Mel Leven, from *101 Dalmatians*

Augusta: Another resignation, this time Suella Braverman, and she stayed resigned (for now*), for "mistakenly" sending official government correspondence by email from her personal account. Did she jump ship or was she pushed? This was recorded after my previous plea although I realised it was bound to be old news in less than 24 hours, which turned out to be even more correct than I had anticipated.

Suella de Vil, The ERG shill.
If they do not scare you,
You took the wrong pill.

To see them all resign is such a thrill.
(Too soon?)
Suella.
(Gone)
There's a new fella. (For how long?)
Toryland-fill.

Wokerati

Inspired by: *Paparazzi*, Lady Gaga

Augusta: The stories in the dying days of Liz Truss' came so thick and fast I didn't have time or energy to record all the parodies that I had written. This was one that I wrote after Suella Braverman faced up to Yvette Cooper in the House of Commons and threw out the apparent slur of 'Tofu eating, Guardian reading, wokerati'. Coining the term 'wokerati' might end up being Braverman's longest lasting legacy.

If you're not a Tory fan,
Eat tofu, and get called a leftie,
You're woka-, wokerati.

Maybe, read The Guardian,
Salad bar you eat that, sorry,
You're woka-, wokerati.

Liz Atrussities

Inspired by: *Bare Necessities*, Terry Gilkyson, from *The Jungle Book*
Augusta: I started writing this a few days before she resigned, but finished it as news of the Russian hacking scandal emerged.

Look at the Liz Attrusities,
Was simply not PM at ease,
She never had more worries or such strife.
You've seen her, stare and blink and freeze,
The Russian neighbours press for sleaze.
But Rish still brings austerities to life.

Fracking Hell Medley

Inspired by: *Don't Look Back in Anger*, Oasis; Return of the Mack, Mark Morrison and *Back to Life*, Soul II Soul

Augusta: More lunacy from Liz Truss as she lifted the ban on fracking which had been a 2019 Conservative manifesto pledge. It was another one of her disastrous ideas to address the Cost of Living Crisis and rising energy prices, which had no grounds in reality. When Rishi Sunak took office he restored the ban almost immediately. I wrote this for the environmental episode of The Strange Mole Show so with extra thanks to Ian for his suggestion of Return of the Frack.

And so fracking can wait,
We know it brings hate,
So we're blocking, don't cry.
The ground won't slide away,
And we won't frack in Lanca(shire),
We heard you say.

(3 years later)

You lied Trussy,
All those times you said you wouldn't though.
You lied Trussy, no surprise, no surprise.

Return of the frack, yes it is,
U-turns on the frack, oh my god.
Return of the frack, her brain's gone.
Please Lord make them backtrack.

(3 weeks later)

Frack brings strife. Frack's not a reality.

Dear oh dear

Mike: King Charles earned many fans across the country by greeting Liz Truss with "Back again? Dear oh dear"

When before the new king she'll appear,
The thing that she won't want to hear
Is for him to reply,
With a sad sort of sigh,
"Are you back again? Dear, oh dear"

Lettuce Leaf ♪

Inspired by: *Let It Be*, The Beatles

Augusta: 20th October 2022 Liz Truss became the shortest serving Prime Minister in British history, and also failed to outlast a live-streamed lettuce. She had been barely clinging onto power but after the resignation of Suella Braverman and her scathing remarks about the direction of Truss's government it turned into the straw that broke the lettuce's back. Thank you to Deborah Feldman and Ste Grenall for this song suggestion.

Lettuce Leaf, she admits defeat,
Can't compete, she's out on the street.

(Best Before)
She speaks no words of wisdom, just fantasy.
(And farce for 44 days)

Now a broken half-arsed Party.
I think that we can all agree.
There is one clear answer.
Let it be.

*[You'll need to watch the video to see
what my dream was.
Hint: It doesn't include sending refugees to Rwanda.]*

Rishi, Rishi, Rishi, Rishi (Take Two) ♪
Inspired by: *Ruby*, The Kaiser Chiefs

*Augusta: Penny Mordaunt was the first to put her
name forward to replace Liz Truss as Prime Minister,
with the next two figures being the main contenders
and rivals. Rishi Sunak and Boris Johnson. The past
weeks had seen such political chaos but it seemed
almost incomprehensible that Boris Johnson was
somehow back in the running for PM. Rishi Sunak had
delayed declaring his candidacy but once he did he
quickly received more than 100 backers. There were
questions whether Johnson would achieve the required
number as he swiftly returned from yet another
holiday, this time in the Caribbean. However, he did
not officially put his name forward and declared
himself out of the running, although not before
declaring that his motivation was the good of the
party.*

Moments before the deadline of 2pm Monday 24th October Penny Mordaunt pulled out having not received enough backers and Rishi Sunak became leader of the party. Following a meeting with the King the next day Rishi Sunak became Prime Minister without a single vote being cast by the Conservative members or general public. I wrote this, still fuming that Sunak was able to hold the office of Prime Minister having broken the lockdown rules and been fined, not to mention the many billions of pounds lost under his chancellorship. 25th October 2022.

Rishi, Rishi, Rishi, Rishi
How long till you resign?
(Christmas?)
Well do ya, do ya, do ya,
Forget that you were fined?
(Small change)

Whata, whata, is your legacy?
Lost billions in your job.
(40 and counting)
Rishi, Rishi, Rishi, Rishi,
Some think that you're a …
(Oops. Trussy, help me out)

Liz Truss: A disgrace.
(Thought so)

Christmas Bonus
Two extra songs that feature in The Strange Mole Show season 3, one touching on the ever-increasing worry of Avian Flu spread in wild and captive birds, and the other on a familiar subject as the water companies continue to contaminate our coasts and waterways.

Little Turkey
Inspired by: *Little Donkey*, Eric Boswell

Little turkey, not so perky,
Flu it must be here.
Little turkey, head is jerky,
Incinerate my dear.

(Good time to go veggie)

We Saw Three Shits
Inspired by: *I Saw Three Ships*, traditional carol

We saw three shits come floating by,
A sewage day, the price you pay,
For private gits they're gloating, why?
They'll cash their cheques in the morning.

(Happy Christmas bonus)

Looking Forward

Mike: The postponed National Rejoin March took place on 22nd October 2022, amidst the shambles of Fantasy Economics which had started with Brexit, I was on holiday by then but it had to be October 22nd so that Terry Reintke MEP could attend, (as she had the European Greens Conference the week before). This was all my fault really, because I had invited Terry to the March in the first place. In the event Guy Verhofstadt came with her as well, which all raised the profile of the March. I was by then in Bosnia

Herzegovina. (Local comment: "Our Government is chaotic – but at least we're not as bad as the UK"). I sent a 3-minute video which was well-received when played in Parliament Square, and you can see that video by scanning this QR code.
This chapter includes material written for the pre-March livestream event

Twelve Stars on the Flag ♪ ♪

Inspired by: *Football's Coming Home,* Frank Skinner and David Baddiel and Lightning Seeds

Mike: This was suggested by Peter Corr of "UK Rejoin the EU". I wrote the lyrics and the song was recorded by Pat Hart. Then Peter Corr made a great video which was aired to great

*effect on "Britannia Waives the Rules" YouTube and
also "UK Rejoin the EU".*

*Commentary "This is good news for the whole
nation"*

"We are a creative people, we are positive"

It's coming home. It's coming home. It's coming.
UK's coming home.

*"We're going to go on to greater things, to greater
things, to greater things"*

It's coming home. It's coming home. It's coming.
UK's coming home.

It's coming home. It's coming home. It's coming.
UK's coming home.

It's coming home. It's coming home. It's coming.
UK's coming home.

It's coming home. It's coming home. It's coming.
UK's coming home.

Everyone seemed to know the score.
They saw it all before.
They just knew.
Were so sure.
That we're gonna throw it away,
It was done as they say,
"Gotta do it my way,"
But I remember -
Had enough of blag,
Always saw this coming,
Twelve stars on the flag,
UK for Rejoining.

So many steps, so many talks,

But all those Rejoin walks
Give you hope
Through the talks,
And so, I see that
Treaty we have,
With a tariff-free zone,
And the customs are done,
With Customs Union,

Twelve stars on the flag,
Finally, we're seeing
Rejoin's in the bag.
Kindly start the cheering.
    Commentary "UK has done it – finally, Rejoined
    They've Rejoined the EU – what a result"
    "Good old EU"
    "You looked after the star"
    "Good old UK"
    "UK has got its place back"
You know that was then.
And it will be again.

It's coming home. It's coming. UK's coming home.
It's coming home. It's coming home. It's coming.
UK's coming home.
    Commentary "UK has done it "–
It's coming home. It's coming home. It's coming.
UK's coming home. It's coming home.
It's coming home. It's coming.
UK's coming home. It's coming home.
It's coming home. It's coming.

Twelve stars on the flag,
'Rasmus is our buddy.
Let me pack my bag.
Live and work and study. (It's coming home).
Twelve stars on the flag. (It's coming home).
(It's coming).
End the right-wing fiction.
(UK coming home). (It's coming home).
Borders not a drag.
(It's coming home). (It's coming).
Trade with no more friction.
(UK coming home). (It's coming home).
Twelve stars on the flag.
(It's coming home). (It's coming).
More co-operation.
(UK coming home). (It's coming home).
Now we'll wave our flag.
(It's coming home). (It's coming).
European Nation. (UK coming home).

Sweet EU Time

Inspired by: *Sweet Caroline,* Neil Diamond
Mike: Written for the National Rejoin March.

How it began, we can recall the lying,
But then we saw them growing strong.
There was Farage,
And Johnson picked his option,
Who'd have believed he'd speak so wrong?

Lies, spreading lies,

Reaching out, touching them, touching who?

Sweet EU time,
Good times never seemed so good.
I've been inclined
To believe they never would.
But now I
Look at the Deal, Brexit don't seem so clever,
We think it's crap in '22.
And when it hurts,
Hurting hits all the U.K.,
We are so hurt we've left EU.

Lies, spreading lies,
Reaching out, touching them, touching who?

Sweet EU time -
Good times never seemed so good.
I've been inclined
To believe they never would.
Oh no, no.

Sweet EU time -
Good times never seemed so good.
I've been inclined
To believe they never would.

Sweet EU time -
Good times never seemed so good.

We're The Rejoiners

Inspired by: *We Are the Champions,* Queen
Mike: Written for the National Rejoin March.

We have explained
Time after Time;
We have been punished,
But committed no crime;
Of bad mistakes,
Brexit was worst;
But those who voted Leave,
If they were fooled,
They were not the first.

And we mean to go on and on and on and on.......

We're the Rejoiners, my friends,
And we'll keep campaigning till the end,
We're the Rejoiners,
We're the Rejoiners,
No time for Brexit,
'Cause we're the Rejoiners of EU.

Not everyone knew
How bad Brexit would go;
It brought down trade and fortune
And everything that goes with it;
What a shit show!
It's been no Sunlit Uplands,
No cards held by Leave;
We know it's a challenge before
We Rejoin EU.

We will achieve.

And we mean to go on and on and on and on..........

We're the Rejoiners, my friends,
And we'll keep campaigning till the end.
We're the Rejoiners,
We're the Rejoiners,
No time for Brexit,
'Cause we're the Rejoiners of EU

We're the Rejoiners, my friends,
And we'll keep campaigning till the end.
We're the Rejoiners,
We're the Rejoiners,
No time for Brexit,
'Cause we're the Rejoiners,
Flags unfurled.

We'll Be Back In EU

Inspired by: *We Will Rock You,* Queen
Mike: Written for the National Rejoin March.

Brexit was a mess, we never said yes.
Messing up the trade, it's no good for anyone in U.K.
We got egg on our face, it's a big disgrace,
Kicking the can all over the place, and so
We'll be back in EU.
We'll be back in EU.

Brexit was a poke pig, bad gig,
Britain going broke,

Forgot who our friends are one day.
We got hope in our face, we'll state our case,
Waving our banners all over the place.

We'll be back in EU.
Sing it
We'll be back in EU.
Yeah.

Brexit ain't got done, no fun.
No Sunlit Heights,
Shredding up people's rights that day.
We got love in this place and a very strong case.
It's time to take Britain back to the right place, so
We'll be back in EU, yeah, yeah, come on
We'll be back in EU, alright, louder! everybody
We'll be back in EU, one more time
We'll be back in EU.
We'll be back in EU, yeah, yeah, come on
We'll be back in EU, alright, louder! everybody
We'll be back in EU, one more time
We'll be back in EU.

Don't Stop Us Now

Inspired by: *Don't Stop Me Now,* Queen
Augusta: A bonus Queen Rejoin anthem.

Don't stop us now,
We're gonna come back sometime,
We'll break through this wall,
No more ciao ciao,
We wanna bring back good times,

Give the union a call.

So, don't stop us now.
Don't stop us, 'cause we're planning a good time,
We'll shout in the meantime.

A Song of Brexitian Triumph ♪

Inspired by *A Song of Patriotic Prejudice,* Flanders &
Swann

Our Brexit, our Brexit, our Brexit is best.
The experts mistaken, like all of the rest.
  "Typical Tory understatement"

So when you're campaigning, be
careless with spin;
You should not define what you'll do if you win.
Now don't believe experts, and don't believe us,
But look what we wrote on our Brexit red bus.

* "Well, we never said we'd actually fund the NHS, did we""

"You'll live work and study in Europe unchanged"
But if you believe that you must be deranged.
There's no alteration to EU folks' rights;
We'll turn a blind eye to their resulting plights.
Our Brexit, our Brexit our Brexit is best.
The Brexit's world-beating, outclasses the rest.

"Oh, voter id needs physical proof but EU citizens don't need it "

And then Northern Ireland, we said we'd do next,
Which is where as it happens we promised no checks.

- Mike Cashman and Augusta Lees -

We didn't expect that the EC would say
That what we had signed would all come into play.
Our Brexit was brilliant, so give it a clap.
If we chuck out the Protocol, call it a wrap.

"Three cheers for the DUP for enabling Brexit?"

We don't want to talk about Benefits now.
In fifty years' time we'll be working out how
The Brexit has helped us; I'm sure that we'll find
Some benefits of the non-monetary kind.

We're doing our best at this new Brexit game;
If there are small problems, Remainers to blame.
Or else it's the EC with petty safeguards,
Who didn't admit that we held all the cards.
Our Brexit is noble, our Brexit is good,
And clever, expensive and misunderstood.

And all the world over, comparing our Deal.
You'll see that we're confident, that's how we feel;
We argue with experts, we may call a halt,
But be in no doubt that all failure's your fault.
Our Brexit, our Brexit, our Brexit is best.
The Brexit's world-beating, outclasses the rest.

You may think we're wily or naturally bad;
But please do not say so, pay taxes, be glad,

With Brexit, with Brexit, with Brexit we're free.
And the source of the Brexit is Tories
Boris, Tories, Boris and me .....

The Cons Will Go On.

Inspired by: *My Heart Will Go On*
*Mike: The Right didn't seem to have any good tunes,
so I wrote this for committed Brexiters, to fill the gap.*
Every night in my dreams,
Unicorns, Sunlit Fields,
That is how I know we go on.
Far across the oceans,
New trade deals appearing.
We'll all just ignore the pong.
Near, far, with distance no bar.
I believe that the Brexit goes on;
No pain, for what's down the drain,
And imagine we've won,
And the Deal will go on and on.

Lies cannot spoil the time,
But last for a lifetime,
And never admit that we're wrong.
Benefits not needed,
The metrics, let's leave it,
For fifty years isn't too long.

Take Back Control, the Con Troll,
They'll believe that we all will go on.
　　　　(Why do we all go on?)
Once more, we gaslight the poor,
And we're here in control,
And the cons will go on and on.
 We're here, with Protocol tears,
And I know that this mess will go on.
We'll stay, forever this way,

They're duped by the deal and
This mess will go on and on.

*Augusta: I worked with Mike to prepare a set of songs
for the National Rejoin March livestream event on
20th August 2022, ahead of the March. These three
collections all explore our feelings, like many others,
towards Brexit.*

French Connections ♪

Inspired by: *Frère Jaques* and *Au Clair de la Lune*
*Mike and Augusta: A joint effort. We each wrote one
verse of this.*

Russian backers, shady hackers.
Leave EU, vote got screwed.
Encircle the hyenas,
And wait for the subpoenas.
Prove them wrong, all day long.
      Those…

Empty words from Tories, mon ami EU.
Hating Brexit stories,
We are missing you.
Leavers lost supporters. Benefits are few.
(Are there any?)
Let's reopen borders, and rejoin EU.

Queen Medley for Rejoin ♪

Inspired by: *We Will Rock You, We Are the Champions, Flash Gordon.*
Augusta: I announced this on the National Rejoin March livestream: "Cashman/Lees original just for today. I think you know what's coming…"

Brexit was a ploy, make a big noise,
Taking to the streets,
Gonna turn it all around someday.

Leave got egg on their face,
A big disgrace.
Tearing our banners all over the place.
EU, we will, back you.
EU, we will, back you.

Brexit hits the old man, poor man
Leavers with their lies,
We were robbed and fleeced that day,
We got hope in our face, we'll state our case,
Waving our banners all over the place.
EU we will back you.
EU we will back you.

'Cause we're the Rejoiners, your friends.
And we'll keep campaigning till the end.
EU we champion. EU we champion.
No time for Leavers, 'cause we're the Rejoiners,
Flags unfurled.
Newsflash, ah-ah, Brexit failed every one of us.
(Unless you've got offshore bank accounts)

We're Coming Home / Sweet EU Time ♪

Inspired by: *Football's Coming Home,* David Baddiel, Frank Skinner and The Lightning Seeds; and *Sweet Caroline,* Neil Diamond
Augusta: A nod to the most feel-good story of the summer as the England Lionesses brought football home at the European Championships.

Twelve stars on the flag,
Fuels Remainers' dreaming.
Six years start to drag,
But Rejoin marchers beaming.

We were part of it then and we could be again,
('Cause guess what?)
It's coming home, we're coming home, it's coming.
UK's coming home.
We're not alone, we will Remoan, we're coming,
UK's coming home…for

Sweet EU time,
Good times never seemed so good.
(Or Brexit quite so bad)
3 PMs resigned,
Full of cons and more falsehoods.
It's our time.
Now.

More from Augusta ♪

 Scan this QR code if you would like to see some more recent songs from Augusta.

More from Mike ♪

 And scan this QR code if you would like to see some more recent videos from Mike.

Please Write a Review!

We hope you enjoyed this book. Please leave a review online – for example on Amazon or Etsy.

As a small independent publisher, Viewdelta Press is very dependent on readers who love our work to
 spread the word. So, if you enjoyed the book, please say so, in order that others can discover the books too. Find all our other books with this QR code.

We can keep you informed of our future projects if you Like our Facebook page:
"Britannia Waives the Rules".

REFERENCE

The first index lists all the pieces in this book, by title, and the second index lists the original titles of the songs which are parodies.

Index of titles

Index of references to original songs

The Authors

MIKE CASHMAN creates serious and satirical items and videos on Brexit and other topics. His satirical works are described on these pages – now including four books and two musical CDs., and the YouTube Channel "Britannia Waives the Rules". Previously he worked in teaching, information systems, project and programme management, and international development.

Being called in to resolve major projects and programmes going wrong – including some Government programmes – has given him a perspective on the UK's approach to Brexit and to Covid; he can also factor in his experience with the project to eradicate Ebola in Sierra Leone.

A speaker at the National Rejoin March, he is available as a speaker or panellist on a variety of topics.

He is married with 4 children and 12 grandchildren.

Mike Cashman
with 3 books and 2 CDs

MIKE AND AUGUSTA are both thrilled to be collaborating with songs for the National Rejoin March liveset and in preparing this book.

AUGUSTA LEES is a classically trained pianist and singer who was first driven to writing political parody when her more usual performances stopped due to lockdown.

What started as a couple of songs has got a little bit out of hand. Due to the Government's terrible pandemic response and her medical vulnerability she continues to avoid catching Covid-19, so can be found frequently lamenting the state of the nation through song via Twitter @augustalees and YouTube, Augusta Lees.

Thanks to Felici Opera she has been able to continue some of her more usual performing with opportunities to do concerts in outside venues, and Augusta was pleased to be able to do some recording with the English Chamber Choir, and online videos with Peregrina EnChantica.

When not making parodies or performing, Augusta teaches the next generation of pianists and singers.

Augusta Lees
Photography:
Christina Lees

More about our work

Please scan these QR codes to learn more.

 Are you looking for a speaker or a panellist for your event?

 Brexit's a Musical Trick" CD / USB ♪

 I Don't Beg Pardon" CD / USB ♪

 Public Comments on our Previous Books

 Viewdelta Press and Charity

 Some Amazon Reviews of our books

A Selection from our Recent Online Reviews

Adam Fowle - Thank you for bringing some satirical sunlight to these shady times. (Come Fly Mask Free)

Dr Alison George - So beautiful, so utterly tragic.
(Covid's in the Air)

All Shorts - Very good bud (Discovering What Brexit was for)

Dr Amir Khan - Love it! (Augusta's version of his Waterfalls)

Andy Hydes - It seems bizarre to hear your angelic voice dishing out those acerbic lyrics. Spot on as always.
(Hit the Road and Pack)

Barry Webber - The very best satire and parody is based in truth and that is why the angry extreme right wing Brexiteers will never be able to match the intelligent and witty monologues you are so skilled at creating Mike. It's amazing how much you can include in under 3 minutes! (This Septic Isle)

Betty Swallocks - One of your best (The Donald Went Down to Georgia)

Billy Mac - I thought this guy was for real at first. So effin funny. Great Job. (Brexit is Going Fine – Lord Toritori)

Bobby - Someone give this lady an OBE for the real truths of the country. (How Does he Survive?)

Chris Fisher – Augusta Lees, that was something brilliant (National Rejoin March songs)

Christiane Coughlan - You are a man of many talents. So good! (When the Covgiants Came)

Christopher Spencer of **Cold War Steve** - Brilliant!
(Hit the Road)

Dr Dan Goyle - Love this. Clever lyrics and a beautiful voice. (Apologise)

Dave Stott - Once again the awesomeness that is Augusta Lees hits so hard on the nose there's a danger of a brain injury.
(Hey Rishi)

Declan O Keeffe - "Journey wherever they might to seek the true benefit of Brexit". Lmfao. This is comedy gold. (World King Boris and the Quest for the Sacred Benefits of Brexit)

Dillie Keane - I particularly liked "Putrefied Words of Dribble" (Edward Leigh)

Dream Dancer - Impressive voice-over. Sounded as if you had hired John Cleese. (World King Boris and the Quest for the Sacred Benefits of Brexit)

Ellie D. Violet - Mike, this was bloody brilliant! (Brexit Human Impact Scale)

@flyingfaeries - Just when the flame of my anger starts to fade Augusta reignites it with a musical commentary that I salute and off we go again to fight the battle for decency in government. (U-turns)

Graham Sims - Nice one, Mike. Your sparkle helps to wash away the dull day-in-day-out tedium of Johnson and his tame media! (The Shit Hits the Fans)

Irene Tosetti MD - This is amazing! Bravissima. (ABBA Medley)

Klaus Wassermann - Brilliant analogy Mike, just laughed myself to tears - (World King Boris Gets Arms and Legs Chopped off).

Matt Green - Lovely Work! (SpAd Day)

Meg - I laugh on the outside, but cry on the inside. (Close to Poo)

Peter Prado - Brilliant as usual. Superb voice, a new Victoria Wood with your parodies. (Come Fly MP)

René van Baren - Sarcastic, no doubt. Spot on, even less doubt. Superb, guaranteed. (Is There Anybody There?)

RK Hodkinson - Another gem from the First Lady of musical satire. (Hit the Road)

Dr Sarah Ali - Superb you are a genius #BanksyOnAPiano (How Much is that Doggie?)

Ste Greenall from **Black Cat Radio** - I'd add Augusta Lees as Minister for Magnificent Parodies. It's a new role; but a vital one. To remind us how bad the current lot is.

Dr Trisha Greenhalgh - Magic (ABBA Medley)

William George Fraser - This brought tears to my eyes. I hope I live to see it happen - (UK's Coming Home).

Please write your own review to encourage others to enjoy this book.
